'If sustainability is to become part of the fabric of 21st-century business, we'll need to develop a new generation of leaders who can navigate a range of complex business topics. Roorda and Rachelson provide a detailed roadmap, a clear, concise and compelling guide to what it takes to have an impact in today's business world. It goes beyond the theoretical and dives into the trenches, with real stories about real professionals, punctuated by hands-on insights. This is required reading for anyone seeking to be a change-maker in business.'

Joel Makower, Chairman and Executive Editor, GreenBiz Group

'A must-read for every member of the human race. Why? Unlike any other book on sustainability I have ever read, it is approachable, entertaining, smart, and thought-provoking. It argues compellingly that sustainable professionalism is the responsibility of us all and unpacks the basic building blocks of humanity.'

Coro Strandberg, CSR Consultant, Strandberg Consulting, Canada

'Reading Roorda can be complicated – but it is always worthwhile! This manuscript lives up to the brilliant level of thought we expect of him. The internationalization of this addition by Rachelson is highly successful. There are inspiring stories here and key insights into becoming an effective sustainability professional – may this small book make a big difference in your practice.'

Peter Blaze Corcoran, Research Fellow, Earth Charter Center for Education for Sustainable Development, University for Peace, Costa Rica

'This timely book astutely integrates the best insights from predecessors including Steven Covey, David Brooks, and Jeffrey Sachs. The authors provide a set of self-directed stepping stones for those who aspire to not only "be the change they seek in others" but to dynamically institutionalize change to serve humankind within a nurtured and nurturing Planet Earth.'

Michael J. Lenaghan, Professor, Miami Dade College and Board Chair, Service for Peace, USA

'The inspiring stories from the professionals that Roorda and Rachelson have brought to life in this fascinating new book create an important antidote for uneasy times and an effective guidebook for sustainability professionals, aspiring millennials, and any reader yearning for smarter uses of precious planetary resources. It just might help us accomplish a soft landing for civilization, before it's too late.'

Joel Solomon, Chairman of Renewal Funds, Canada

THE SEVEN COMPETENCES OF THE SUSTAINABLE PROFESSIONAL

The Seven Competences of the Sustainable Professional shows how every professional can contribute to sustainable development. Through real-life stories told by a range of professionals, each illustrating a sustainability competence, this book provides a practical guide to help professionals realize their sustainability potential. Together, these competences form an accessible framework that is explained in practical terms. Readers are able to check their own sustainability competence level and make plans for personal development at each stage of the book.

There are dozens of books explaining how companies and organizations should work decently, dealing with topics like corporate social responsibility (CSR), sustainable entrepreneurship, and corporate governance. There is an equally large number of books that describe how individuals should behave in their private lives, for instance, by buying healthy food, using energy-saving equipment, showering with less water, and switching off lights in empty rooms. However, this is the first book to provide individual professionals with a clear framework to enable them to act in a sustainable way in their workplace, be they the CEO, CFO, manager, or office worker.

NIKO ROORDA is a leading consultant and author in Social Development and CSR. He has coached more than 50 universities and other organizations in the development and implementation of SD-related strategies and policies.

ANOUCHKA RACHELSON is Professor in the Department of World Languages, Miami Dade College, USA.

THE SEVEN COMPETENCES OF THE SUSTAINABLE PROFESSIONAL

DEVELOPING BEST PRACTICE IN A WORK SETTING

Niko Roorda
with Anouchka Rachelson

Routledge
Taylor & Francis Group

LONDON AND NEW YORK

First published 2018
by Routledge
2 Park Square, Milton Park, Abingdon, Oxon OX14 4RN

and by Routledge
711 Third Avenue, New York, NY 10017

Routledge is an imprint of the Taylor & Francis Group, an informa business

British Library Cataloguing-in-Publication Data
A catalogue record for this book is available from the British Library

Library of Congress Cataloging-in-Publication Data
Names: Roorda, Niko, author. | Rachelson, Anouchka, author.
Title: The seven competences of the sustainable professional :
    developing best practice in a work setting / Niko Roorda with
    Anouchka Rachelson.
Description: Abingdon, Oxon ; New York, NY : Routledge, 2018. |
    Includes bibliographical references and index.
Identifiers: LCCN 2017048593 | ISBN 9780815381235 (hbk) |
    ISBN 9780815381303 (pbk)
Subjects: LCSH: Sustainable development. | Performance.
Classification: LCC HC79.E5 R649 2018 | DDC 650.1—dc23
LC record available at https://lccn.loc.gov/2017048593

ISBN: 978-0-8153-8123-5 (hbk)
ISBN: 978-0-8153-8130-3 (pbk)
ISBN: 978-1-351-12263-4 (ebk)

Typeset in Minion Pro
by Apex CoVantage, LLC

CONTENTS

———

CONTENTS

Introduction
By Niko Roorda

This book fills a gap.

There is a lot of literature about how to behave in a sustainable and socially responsible manner, but something has been missing.

On the one hand, there are dozens of books explaining how companies and other organizations should act decently. Such books tell you about corporate social responsibility (CSR), sustainable entrepreneurship, and corporate governance (i.e. the behavior of owners, boards, and managers). You will find books discussing the responsibility of organizations toward the environment as well as their employees, procurers, and customers. Yet others investigate the responsibilities of financial institutions, governments, and society in general with regards to sustainability.

On the other hand, there are perhaps just as many books describing how individuals should behave in their private lives as responsible customers, for example, by buying locally grown food and clothes that were not produced by child labor or wage slavery. You can find guides on purchasing energy-efficient equipment, such as low-flow showerheads and toilets, and books urging you to change your daily behavior like switching off lights and printing on both sides. There is also literature on becoming a more responsible citizen by donating money to charities, volunteering for non-profit organizations (NGOs), being open to other people's values and cultures, and participating in elections.

Between these two groups of books – those for professional organizations and those for individuals in their private lives – I discovered an open space. How about individuals working as professionals? Many of them have paid jobs as managers or as employees in a company, non-profit organization, or government department. Others work as independent professionals, for example, as artists, consultants, contractors, store clerks, etc. Finally, some may serve as volunteers and still act as experienced professionals.

The roles of these professionals are extremely important because:

Every decision made by a company, government, or organization is ultimately taken by human beings.

All actions undertaken by a company, government, or organization are always performed by human beings.

For all of those people – *individuals at work* – I have written this book.

EVERY PROFESSIONAL CAN CONTRIBUTE TO SUSTAINABLE DEVELOPMENT

Sustainably competent professionals are what our society needs – in huge quantities, in all kinds of professions, and across every thinkable sector: industry, service, finance, government, healthcare, education, farming, fishing, and forestry. We need them in multinational companies, small and medium enterprises (SMEs), family-owned businesses, commercial companies, NGOs, and informal associations.

You can be a sustainably competent professional at *every level* within an organization, regardless of whether you are a CEO or a CFO, a middle manager, a specialist, a salesperson, or an assembly line worker. *Every professional can contribute to sustainable development.*

To prove this, I have developed an instrument that may help you find out how you can significantly contribute to sustainable development. The instrument is called RESFIA+D, and it consists of seven competences. Six of them are 'generic' competences, which means that they are relevant for every professional. The seventh is called 'disciplinary.' Actually, it is an infinitely large group of competences linked to all kinds of specific sectors and professions because there is potentially an unlimited number of professions.

The *Seven Competences of the Sustainable Professional* are shown in Figure 1.1. As you can see, each of the six generic competences is expressed in terms of three types of concrete professional achievements.

RESFIA+D: The Seven Competences of the Sustainable Professional	
Competence *R*: Responsibility *A sustainably competent professional bears responsibility for his or her own work.*	**Competence *E*: Emotional intelligence** *A sustainably competent professional empathizes with the values and emotions of others.*
R1. Create a stakeholder analysis on the basis of the consequence scope and the consequence period	E1. Recognize and respect his or her own values and those of other people and cultures
R2. Take personal responsibility	E2. Distinguish between facts, assumptions and opinions
R3. Be held personally accountable with respect to society *(transparency)*	E3. Cooperate on an interdisciplinary and transdisciplinary basis
Competence *S*: System orientation *A sustainably competent professional thinks and acts from a systemic perspective.*	**Competence *F*: Future orientation** *A sustainably competent professional works and thinks on the basis of a perspective of the future.*
S1. Think from systems – flexibly zoom in and out on issues, i.e. thinking analytically and holistically in turn	F1. Think on different time scales – flexibly zoom in and out on short and long term approaches
S2. Recognize flaws in the fabric and sources of vigor in systems; have the ability to use the sources of vigor	F2. Recognize and utilise non-linear processes
S3. Think integrally and chain oriented	F3. Think innovatively, creatively, out of the box
Competence *I*: personal Involvement *A sustainably competent professional has a personal involvement in sustainable development.*	**Competence *A*: Action skills** *A sustainably competent professional is decisive and capable of acting.*
I1. Consistently involve sustainable development in the own work as a professional (sustainable attitude)	A1. Weigh up the unweighable and make decisions
I2. Passionately work towards dreams and ideals	A2. Deal with uncertainties
I3. Employ his or her conscience as the ultimate yardstick	A3. Act when the time is right, and not go against the current: 'action without action'
+ Competence *D*: Disciplinary Competences *A sustainably competent professional possesses a rich variety of competences for sustainable development that are specific to his or her profession.*	
D1, D2, D3, ... : To be specified separately for all kinds of sectors, disciplines, professions, etc.	

Figure 1.1 *Overview of RESFIA+D*

RESFIA+D is a tool that can be used in several ways as Chapter 14 at the end of the book will show you: to design personal development plans, to facilitate professional training in human resources within a company, or to develop curricula in institutions of higher education.

While the RESFIA+D competence model was being used in these various ways for a number of years, it became clear that readers felt a need for concrete examples from real people who expressed one or more of those competences in an interesting or even an excellent way – *role models* acting in real life.

This book offers these examples. The competences themselves are described only briefly. More space is dedicated to the stories of *real* professionals, interviewed either by me (Niko) or by my co-author, Anouchka Rachelson. In some cases, the exemplary stories were written by the professionals themselves and only slightly edited by us.

THE THEORETICAL FOUNDATION OF RESFIA+D

The science behind RESFIA+D is treated only succinctly in this book, as it primarily targets professionals in all kinds of settings. It is a practitioners' book, not a scientific publication. Many practitioners may not really be interested in theoretical considerations. However, if you want to read more about the theoretical details, you can do two things:

> You can visit my website at https://niko.roorda.nu. More specifically, you can go to the RESFIA+D section, https://niko.roorda.nu/management-methods/resfia-d. There you will find interesting details that are not in this book. Please take a look!

If that is still not enough, you can read all about the scientific backgrounds of the RESFIA+D model in a chapter that I wrote for a different book called 'Management for Sustainable Development' (for details: see the References and Weblinks, at the end of this book).

LANGUAGE EDITIONS

This book is part of a larger project. The goal is to have 'The Seven Competences of the Sustainable Professional' published in multiple languages and in many parts of the world. The English edition is the second version. The first edition was in Dutch (*De Zeven Competenties van de Duurzame Professional*, Garant, 2015).

Presenting a new edition for a specific language or region is not just a matter of translating an earlier one. That would not work. If the professionals who tell their stories are to be true role models, they have to appeal to the readers in the target region. In the Dutch edition, the 'heroes' (as I call them) are Dutch or Belgian. For the English edition, primarily focusing on North America, nearly all stories had to be replaced by case studies of American 'heroes.' My co-author, Anouchka Rachelson, a professor at Miami Dade College in Florida, undertook this immense task. Thanks to her, we now have an excellent set of stories that will inspire readers in the US, Canada, and everywhere else where people read English books. A Spanish edition aiming both at Spain and Latin America is underway.

If you have any ideas or opportunities to promote the development of an edition in another language or for another region, please let me know. You can find my contact data on my website.

CHAPTER ONE
One of my heroes

Vita Vanderbilt, age 27, is one of my heroes: I am deeply impressed by what she has achieved, and I will tell you why.

For a few years, Vita has been a registered nurse in a large, modern hospital. In the years that she has been employed there, she gradually started realizing that hardly any cases of child abuse were ever reported in her hospital. At first, she was okay with that; it gave her the impression that child abuse did not often occur in the city where she lived and worked. However, over the years, she began to find it more and more peculiar because in other hospitals, even those in the same region, cases of child abuse were regularly reported. Those cases concerned physical or mental violence, negligence, and even sexual abuse – often by the victim's own parents. It was difficult to believe that, in the vicinity of the hospital Vita was working, the number of abused children was really considerably lower than in the rest of the country. There had to be another explanation! Either the hospital staff was not as skilled in recognizing child abuse, or perhaps her colleagues had other reasons for not reporting more cases.

Whatever the reasons, it was quite serious. When children arrive in a hospital after having been abused, what the medical staff does may literally be a matter of life and death. If the caretakers only dress wounds and apply casts to broken bones and then send the little patients back home, they fail dramatically.

Vita initiated conversations about the problem with her colleagues in the emergency unit. Naturally, they were the ones most qualified to recognize suspicious injuries and bruises, for example, on the head, the arms, or the genitals. Most doctors and nurses Vita talked to did not seem worried, however. What you don't see, you don't know! Besides, from the discussions Vita had with them, it became clear that many of her colleagues considered it too much of a hassle. Even one single report of child abuse produced a ton of work. Others told her that, now and then, they had indeed noticed signs of child abuse, but they had no idea how or where to report this. Some doctors and nurses even appeared scared: What if an accused father filed a complaint against the informant, or worse, what if he stalked the nurse or doctor outside the hospital?

Nevertheless, some of Vita's colleagues – a few doctors, a hospital psychologist, and some nurses – agreed with her: This was not right. They formed a working group and investigated how other hospitals dealt with these kinds of situations. They also designed a training program for their colleagues. How do you recognize child abuse? In which cases are broken arms, bruises, burning wounds, scars, or injured genitals indications of abuse? How can you see through stories such as "Yes, she fell down the stairs"? What do you do when you suspect child abuse? All such issues were adopted in the training program. Meetings with the hospital board were held to design a clear procedure for reporting cases of abuse. A standard report form, which had been in use in other hospitals for several years, was finally introduced.

The group worked hard to disseminate the news about the reporting procedure and its relevance. Resistance came from many doctors and nurses, but the group, supported by the hospital board, persevered. More and more colleagues grew enthusiastic. Now, a few years later, several cases of child abuse are reported weekly. Thanks to this, every year at least 100 children are saved from a violent home situation or – in a number of cases – from death.

REAL PROFESSIONALS AND THEIR COMPETENCES

When I heard about what Vita had done, I was deeply impressed. She is a young woman, pretty much at the start of her professional career. She has not been assigned a managerial position. She is just one of those thousands of nurses in this huge hospital, but she minds what she sees – or rather, what she does *not* see. However, that was not all. When she thought that something was wrong, she started an initiative. She did not rest until – in spite of all kinds of resistance – she found allies with whom she could take this on.

For me, this example is especially wonderful because it proves that everyone, in whatever field, can do something genuinely relevant. Vita put something in motion in the interest of *people*. Others have, thanks to their profession, been able to act on behalf of *nature* or for the environment. These people prove their genuine professionalism by doing more than they ought to do based on their job descriptions. These men and women act just because they think they should. They all contribute, each in their own way, to sustainable development. They show one or more extraordinary competences: skills that make them excellent professionals.

I will describe to you a few of the competences Vita showed when she struggled for the rights of injured children. One such competence was: she listened to the voice of her own consciousness. She did not uncritically perform the tasks that had been ordered by her superiors. She thought for herself about her job and her working environment, and she took the initiative because she thought she had to. Somewhere further in this book I will show you that this is an excellent example of a competence that is described as:

Employ his or her conscience as the ultimate yardstick.

In the explanation I will give you in the corresponding chapter, you will read: "You exhibit exemplary behavior and leadership thanks to your openly conscious approach," which is exactly what Vita did. Although she did not have a management position, she established leadership by getting first a small group on her side, next the hospital board, and finally a large majority of the entire staff. Another competence Vita showed was:

Personal responsibility

She did not hide behind her formal job description or behind the assignments and opinions of her superiors. She felt personally involved in what was going on in "her" hospital. There, too, she proved herself an excellent (sustainable) professional.

COMPETENCES FOR SUSTAINABILITY

In the chapter about the competence "responsibility," you will read: "Based on your personal responsibility, you work continuously on the improvement of activities, thus contributing to sustainable development."

Perhaps it surprises you to read the term "sustainable development" here. Does combating child abuse have anything to do with sustainable development? Sure! With what is described as "social sustainability." Besides that, there is "ecological sustainability," aiming at nature and the environment, and "economic sustainability," dealing with economic stability, sustainability of companies, and prosperity of people and communities. Together they form the well-known triangle "people," "planet," and "profit." I will return to this later.

Vita is one of my heroes. Look, I myself work as a professional on sustainable development. I am paid to do so. I coach people and organizations toward sustainability, and I write books about it. So for me, it is natural to contribute to sustainability, but for Vita it is not natural: her job description does not mention it at all. And yet, she does it: she delivers a magnificent and unique contribution in her case for social sustainability.

Her example inspired me to write this book because she illustrates how someone in an "ordinary" position in a random organization can play an exceptional role for the sake of our society. Her example proves that everybody can do that – on the condition that you truly want it, and that you keep your eyes wide open to see what can be accomplished. *Everyone, no matter what profession, can contribute to sustainability.* You too, dear reader!

You don't believe me? Read on. You will see the true stories of more of my heroes. Together, they will prove what I say. You will see.

By the way, the name of Vita Vanderbilt has been changed at her request. It is not her real name; however, most of the names you will see are real. Only a few people could not or did not want their names in this book.

THE CIVILIAN, THE CONSUMER, AND THE PROFESSIONAL

Various sources – e.g. books and presentations – distinguish two kinds of roles of individuals: the civilian and the consumer. You may be familiar with it. Personally, I recognize this idea clearly. When I think about responsible behavior as a citizen, driving 65 mph on a highway seems like a pretty fair speed to me, and eating healthy food appears important. However, when I am in my car, it feels good to drive faster, and in the supermarket, I don't just buy responsible food but also those nice and shiny, sweet or spicy snacks. But maybe your mind is stronger than mine.

It is a constant struggle: the sensible citizen versus the easily tempted consumer. Actually, both have opportunities to act sustainably. The citizen may vote conscientiously and participate in discussions to support civic organizations. The consumer may carefully use electricity and water or buy fair trade products, sustainable fish, and FSC-certified wood – and never more than needed.

However, there is a third role: the professional. This book addresses professionals – that is to say: you. It is true that many books and websites dealing with sustainability in the professional world have been introduced. Nearly without exception, they are about companies and organizations *as a whole*. Nevertheless, in the end, anything those businesses or institutions do is the work of separate individuals. Those professionals ranking high or low in the organization, from CEOs and top managers to production employees, administrative staff, nurses, or janitors – all matter. About them, the individual professionals, not much has been written yet. That is the reason for this book, in which you will find examples that will inspire you in your role as a professional. Amidst somber stories about the economy and the environment, these will bring you hope. Yes, hope, because you will see that you yourself are able to work for a better world – you – personally.

Before I forget, on the final pages of this book, after the concluding chapter, I have inserted a list of relevant web links and a glossary. It is always nice to know this right from the start and not to discover it at the end.

RESFIA+D: THE SEVEN COMPETENCES OF THE SUSTAINABLE PROFESSIONAL

The competences I will tell you about are called "RESFIA+D." That is an abbreviation. The first six characters, "R-E-S-F-I-A," represent general competences, i.e. those you may expect from any professional. The seventh, "D," is short for "Disciplinary." That is to say: related to separate professions or disciplines. At the end of the book, in Chapter 14, I will return to RESFIA+D in the shape of a quick self-test that you can fill out in order to learn more about yourself as a professional. Here, at the end of Chapter 1, I present to you a brief overview so that you know what to expect. Right after this overview, in Chapter 2, I will start with the first set of competences, belonging to the "R" of "Responsibility." Here is the overview. Please notice the initials.

Responsibility – A sustainably competent professional bears responsibility for his or her own work.

- *Create a stakeholder analysis on the basis of the consequence scope and the consequence period*
- *Take personal responsibility*
- *Be held personally accountable with respect to society (transparency)*

Emotional intelligence – A sustainably competent professional empathizes with the values and emotions of others.

- *Recognize and respect his or her own values and those of other people and cultures*
- *Distinguish between facts, assumptions, and opinions*
- *Cooperate on an interdisciplinary and transdisciplinary basis*

Systems orientation – A sustainably competent professional thinks and acts from a systemic perspective.

- *Think about systems: flexibly zoom in and out of issues, i.e. thinking analytically and holistically in turn*
- *Recognize flaws in the fabric and sources of vigor in systems; have an ability to use the sources of vigor*
- *Think integrally and chain-oriented*

Future orientation – A sustainably competent professional works and thinks on the basis of a perspective of the future.

- *Think in different time scales: flexibly zoom in and out of short- and long-term approaches*
- *Recognize and utilize non-linear processes*
- *Think innovatively, creatively, and out of the box*

Involvement – A sustainably competent professional is personally involved in sustainable development.

- *Consistently involve sustainable development in his or her own work as a professional (sustainable attitude)*
- *Passionately strive toward dreams and ideals*
- *Employ his or her conscience as the ultimate yardstick*

Action skills – A sustainably competent professional is decisive and capable of acting.

- *Assess the unquantifiable and make decisions*
- *Deal with uncertainties*
- *Act when the time is right, and do not go against the current: "action without action"*

Disciplinary competences. Select which competences are related to your discipline and/or profession.

- . . .
- . . .
- . . .

THE CHAPTERS

You will find the six general competences, RESFIA, in the even-numbered chapters, i.e. in Chapters 2, 4, etc. In between, in the odd-numbered chapters, the focus will be on topics such as: What is sustainable development? What exactly are competences? At which level can one possess the general competences?

The disciplinary competences, which vary by profession, can be found in Chapter 11. Presenting a complete set of such competences would be impossible since there are thousands of different professions; therefore, Chapter 11 offers you a selection of such disciplinary competences.

In my opinion, the set of six general sustainability competences is representative. I will return to this in Chapter 13. If you possess all six, at a fair or even an excellent level, you may truthfully call yourself a *sustainably competent professional*.

Finally, in Chapter 14, you will have the opportunity to assess yourself. Are you a sustainably competent professional? And if so, at which level? Lastly, are you prepared to pledge that you will consistently act as a sustainably competent professional?

CHAPTER TWO
Responsibility

The Competence (Figure 2.1):

A sustainably competent professional takes responsibility for his or her own work.

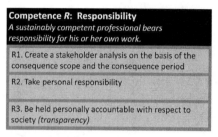

Figure 2.1 *Competence R: Responsibility*

"I take full responsibility." You can read this in the newspaper or hear it on TV. Usually, it means: "I quit my job." You may be watching a politician or a football coach who is resigning.

People who say such a thing have a very limited view of responsibility. To express it even more strongly, it is actually a euphemism for transferring the responsibility to someone else.

In reality, responsibility, of course, is something totally different. Let's say you have the responsibility for a group of elderly patients, or children. Responsibility then means that you do *not* leave, but instead take care of them continuously and, if necessary, defend their interests against those of others. Of course, if you cannot do that anymore, you act responsibly if you transfer your responsibility to someone else.

To take responsibility means standing for what you do and communicating that openly. As a professional, you do that in the first place by investigating conscientiously what kind of consequences your work has, and for whom – in a positive or negative sense. To put it more formally: by discovering *all stakeholders* in your work.

Each of the six general sustainability competences is linked to certain concrete achievements. By realizing such achievements, a professional demonstrates that he or she possesses the related competence. For the competence *Responsibility* the achievements are:

- *Find stakeholders*
- *Take responsibility*
- *Be accountable*

2.1 FIND STAKEHOLDERS

Simone Lopulisa's ideas immediately fell on fertile ground. Simone works for a bank, one of those special banks that have adopted sustainability as their basis or their mission, and really operate accordingly. The bank attaches value to transparency and to dialogues (or relationships) with customers, stakeholders, and society. Probably that was the reason why Lopulisa's plan was immediately embraced. She proposed to perform a stakeholder analysis in a special way.

Who has an interest in what you do as a professional? Your customers, of course, or your students, or perhaps your patients? Maybe your shareholders, managers, colleagues, or employees? Please choose whoever applies to you. Your partner and your children, if you have any. All are obvious stakeholders of your work.

But there is more. Suppose that your work produces annoying noises, or perhaps your visiting customers cause parking problems. In those cases, you create a nuisance for your neighbors. This implies that they, too, have a stake in your work, albeit a negative stake.

Negative stakes may exist in many ways. If you work too hard, your family may suffer from it. If you sell clothing that is produced in China or Bangladesh, there is a chance that you profit from child labor or wage slavery. If you drive to work, you cause emissions and greenhouse gases – even if you use an electric car – and aerosols. Don't get me wrong. This is not an accusation. *Everybody* causes negative effects. You just can't avoid it. Of course, you can strive to minimize them.

The first step in accepting responsibility consists of finding all stakeholders, those with a positive stake – a benefit – and those with a negative one. The next step entails consulting with them, aiming to maximize the positive and minimize or compensate for the negative.

If a company performs a stakeholder analysis, it usually starts with a group of sensitive and experienced staff members discussing who has a stake in what the company is doing. In most cases, the traditional groups will be recognized, e.g. the shareholders and the customers. However, the risk is that there will be "blind spots," causing certain kinds of interests to go unnoticed. Simone Lopulisa proposed to adopt a totally different approach, through which each and all – known and yet unknown – stakeholders would get the opportunity to present themselves. Her strategy was based on *crowdsourcing*.

"This goes far beyond defining the target group," Simone explains. "Crowdsourcing is the online gathering of knowledge and suggestions of a large group of people aiming at creating ideas, solving problems or the creation of a policy. Crowdsourcing makes you – as an organization – look further than just the traditional group of stakeholders. Social media enables you to reach a much larger group of partly yet unknown people and to spread the message fast. The dialogue you start this way is different from what it would have been if you had only communicated with your clients. This 'new group of stakeholders' often delivers refreshing and surprising ideas."

In the summer of 2011, the method was applied for the first time, with the theme "human rights policy." This theme was divided into four parts: fair trade; against child labor; against arms trade; and sustainable energy. Simone placed challenging assertions on a blog, sparking an online discussion. Everyone who wished to participate in redefining the bank's policy was able to join. The bank asked for assistance from social organizations, e.g. Amnesty International, labor unions, Foster Parents Plan, and Cordaid to introduce the process to a lot of people and to invite them to join the discussions. The bank employees were asked to utilize their private networks in order to further enlarge the publicity for this new policy. All in all, this crowdsourcing proved to be highly successful. At the height of the action, 140,000 Twitter users and the bank's own sustainability platform, with 52,000 members, were involved.

The bank used the contributions to the discussion to improve its policy. One of the results was that privacy and freedom of expression became a separate chapter in the human rights policy.

One year later, Lopulisa gave me some advice for those who want to try to do what she has done. "Always respond. Don't make any promises: If you promise to respond to every message, then do so. Be honest, every time you respond. Thank the involved persons in a personal way. Send them feedback about what you have done with their input. Get going with the input you receive, and always inform the involved people if this appears to be impossible, for whatever reason. Crowdsourcing is a tool, not a target in itself: always start from intrinsic motivation. Feel free to invite those who are eager to be involved more than once. Attempt to deepen the online dialogue by continuing it offline."

THE ACHIEVEMENT

You create a stakeholder analysis based on the consequence scope and the consequence period.

This means:

- *You find everyone who is a stakeholder in your work. For each one, you determine what the stake consists of: both the positive and the negative aspects.*
- *For this purpose, you start by determining the consequence scope and the consequence period of all your professional activities.*
- *You consult all stakeholders or their representatives in order to determine their stakes.*
- *You use the conclusions of this analysis and the consultations for the continuous improvement of your work.*

Many of our (positive or negative) stakeholders are perfectly able to defend their own interests, but not all. Little children and those with mental disabilities don't have the ability, or only to a lesser degree. In that case, you don't communicate directly with them but with their representatives: parents, interest groups, the government, or maybe a legal counselor. Can animals be stakeholders? Legally, they can't, as they are not persons according to laws in many countries; however, it is clear that some decisions will have a favorable or an unfavorable impact on certain animals. So yes, animals can be *de facto* stakeholders, and there are organizations defending their interests. How about nature as a whole? "Sure!" is the answer of organizations such as the World Wildlife Fund and the International Union for the Conservation of Nature (IUCN). In other words, a valid stakeholder analysis, one that is comprehensive from a sustainability perspective, can be quite sizeable.

A valuable concept is the **consequence scope**. This is the full extent of persons, organizations, communities, and the environment that experience the consequences of your decisions and activities. Yet, even that is not sufficient.

Sustainable development specifically is not only related to the present but also to the future. Is it possible for people born in or after the year 2050 to be stakeholders of the work we do *now*? Absolutely, beyond any doubt. Taking the interest of these yet to be named individuals into account is definitely a main aspect of our responsibility. However, it is impossible to communicate with them here and now. This means that we should act as their representatives and think about their interests.

The counterpart of the consequence scope is the **consequence period**. That is the time it will take before the consequences of your decisions and actions have fully faded away. Consequence periods can vary. If I choose between a cup of coffee and a cappuccino, the consequence period of my decision may be a quarter of an hour, as afterwards the coffee is gone and forgotten. If the national government decides to construct a transcontinental railroad or a project like the proposed Keystone XL pipeline that would run from Alberta (Canada) to Texas, the consequence period of that decision is at least a full century.

The consequence period of a nuclear plant amounts to hundreds of thousands of years, due to the radioactive waste. Consequence scope and consequence period together form two dimensions: the dimensions of "space" and "time." Together they are helpful to define a natural rule of thumb for making sound decisions.

Directions for a good decision

A decision can only be a good decision:

- *if the advantages and disadvantages for the entire consequence scope are determined and scrupulously weighed in consultation with the stakeholders; and*
- *if it can be reasonably expected that the people at the conclusion of the consequence period will think it was a good decision.*

2.2 TAKE RESPONSIBILITY

Redmond, a leafy suburb of Seattle, Washington, already had two mosques. When Hyder Ali first proposed building a third one, the local Muslim community initially did not understand why another mosque was needed in East Seattle. The two existing ones were predominantly religious places of worship, explains Ali, the mosque's founding president and current board of trustees member. "We, however, wanted a new organization that addressed spiritual, social, cultural needs of the community, which we commonly referred to as 'a place to pray and play.' It was the year 2006, and this was a new idea. We had a vision of inclusiveness, which meant offering positions on the board for both men and women and giving women a choice whether they wanted to worship behind a partition or not. Back then, such an arrangement was not so common."

The new mosque was going to house conference rooms, meeting places, a banquet hall, a café, a gym, and an indoor basketball court, so the facility had to be spacious. It sounded like a great plan, but the community was fragmented. "People didn't understand our vision. They would ask: Why do you want to build it and why so close to an existing mosque?" Ali recalls. "They say it is location, location, and location. The place had to be where people lived." Ali knew that his responsibility as a community leader was to be proactive to avoid further conflict. His non-profit organization, Muslim Association of Puget Sound (MAPS) started renting space in an office building, and Ali set out to convince community members. "There was a huge potential in the community that was not being tapped into. A portion of the community felt disenfranchised . . . We needed an institution that gave this segment 'a platform to pursue their dreams.'"

Ali encountered several challenges. "The community had grown large enough that the city asked us to either find a different location or ask the landlord of the rental facility to make extensive changes to meet city codes . . . After some search, we were lucky to find an ideal place in a perfect location but had two problems. First, we needed to raise an enormous amount of money, which had not been done before. We also did not know if we would be able to sustain such a facility operationally. The second challenge was how to rally the community behind this project. Changing people's social habits is hard. People go where their friends go."

Three years passed. It was 2009, and while MAPS was busy planning the construction of its new mosque and community center, another mosque project on the other side of the country started drawing nationwide attention. Since the 9/11 attacks, public sentiments toward Muslims had changed and the proposed mosque, known as Park51, adjacent to Ground Zero, resulted in considerable conflict as many people were opposed to a mosque so close to the historic site. The incident certainly did not help Ali's cause.

Ali had to weigh his responsibility. Under the existing circumstances, it would have been easier to drop the plans, but when considering the future, he strongly felt that the community in Redmond had a right to a modern, inclusive community center that would meet the needs of all stakeholders. He had been appointed president of the organization, so he felt his duty was to push the plans through and provide his community with the center it deserved.

Looking back, Ali remembers: "You have to be 100% sure that you are doing the right thing. You have to have a vision. We talked to the different stakeholders in the city. Part of our mosque's charter was to be visible and open. We invited the mayors of all the nearby cities. That was in 2010, when the New York controversy was at full blast, and we were a bit impacted. The mayor of Redmond was in favor of having a diverse community, but there was a neighbor who came to the city meeting with a concern about parking and his business. Later, when we addressed his concerns, he withdrew his objection, and we've had a good relationship ever since."

Asked how he and his fellow leadership members addressed the challenges responsibly, Ali responds, "First, through constant communication to the community both in our personal capacity and in formal settings. Also, through building credibility by delivering on what we promised. For example, we said, we would have an elected board, and we held our elections as promised. Finally, through community engagement. For all major decisions, we solicited community feedback and relentlessly articulated the rationale for our decisions. It's important to listen and reflect. You have to balance between listening, and leading with your conviction . . . We also always took the high ground when we felt we were misunderstood or were not treated as we had expected. We did not want others to define who we were, and so did not give up on our vision to appease others."

The new mosque opened in 2011. Aside from serving as a place of worship, it has blossomed into a community center for the people of Redmond, offering robotics and art classes for children, SAT tutoring for high school students, ESL courses for local residents, and opportunities for interfaith activities.

THE ACHIEVEMENT

You accept personal responsibility and act accordingly.

This means:

- *You feel and show personal responsibility for your professional activities and their consequences.*
- *If different professional responsibilities conflict, you weigh them carefully against each other and act accordingly.*
- *You apply this responsibility proactively, by involving current and possible future developments and trends.*
- *Based on your personal responsibility, you strive continuously to improve your activities, thus contributing to sustainable development.*
- *You have to listen, but sometimes you have to lead based on your conviction.*

It may not seem very hard – taking responsibility for your work, and it isn't, as long as your decisions and actions match one another and with what you think is right and enjoyable. However, what if they are not? What if you are forced to make tough decisions when the interests of different stakeholders conflict? It is then that you have to judge critically where your primary responsibility lies and stand for what you do so that those who depend on you know they can rely on you.

Sometimes the distinction between the words "responsibility" and "accountability" are not clear to everyone. However, they are not equal. Responsibility is something that you accept and then carry. It is something that happens inside of you: a decision you make, and after which you act accordingly.

Accountable is what you are to others. Whereas taking responsibility happens inside you, accountability takes place between you and the outside world, and not just in one direction but also in the form of a dialogue. Show what you do: be transparent! That is what the next competence is about.

2.3 BE ACCOUNTABLE: TRANSPARENCY

Herman Betten is the manager of communications at DSM, a large multinational company. DSM is highly active in the field of sustainability and corporate social responsibility (CSR), and Betten is one of the driving forces behind it. "Although I consider myself a financial nerd – I design Excel sheets for pleasure – I am convinced that companies should do more than just make money. They need to exercise social responsibility as well," he wrote on the website About.me.

Hermann is a dedicated person. On behalf of DSM, he took part in a roundtable organized by the British newspaper *The Guardian* together with the *Children's Investment Fund Foundation*, an international non-government organization (NGO). The theme of the meeting was the fourth Millennium Development Goal: reducing global child mortality by two thirds in 2015. The attendees discussed options for public–private cooperation, in which governments and NGOs join forces with companies to combat malnutrition. Betten strongly believes in such combined efforts, including an intensive commitment of DSM. "We take 'people, planet and profit' seriously. We believe that we are capable of helping others solve the world's biggest problems."

Betten has been involved in the annual reports of his company for several years as manager of communications. In recent years, big steps have been taken toward transparency, and this is highly appreciated. "DSM's annual report is very readable, according to the jury, and it is an integral report in which CSR is discussed as the very first item. There is improved information about the dialogue with stakeholders, compared to last year (. . .). The jury is highly impressed by the attention given to the issues in the chapter 'What still went wrong.'"

These are a few of the opening lines in the jury report of the Crystal Awards 2012. In that year, DSM was – just as the year before – the winner of the Crystal, subtitled the 'award for discerning societal reporting.' "Of the three finalists," the jury report continues, "DSM's report has the strongest external orientation. The main themes in the report and their progress have all been placed in a societal context. With the initiative of a Sustainability Advisory Board DSM shows that it sets another step on the path of CSR, and the company also shows which roles each member of the Board fulfills in the societal context. With this 'Walk the Talk' the board sets the example for the rest of the organization."

An annual report of a multinational company such as DSM (in 2012: net turnover 9 billion euros; 23,500 employees on five continents) is not easily prepared. Many people contribute to it, but there has to be one person responsible for the overall design. Betten wrote to me about how the award-winning reporting was developed.

"From 2007 until 2011, I was allowed to design and edit DSM's annual reports. What for me started as a financial report – with a *Triple P* report added to it, prepared by someone else writing about the relations between *people, planet,* and *profit* – ended as a fully integrated annual report which served all stakeholders. In the last decade, the influence of businesses on many aspects of the global society has grown considerably. This increased influence brings forth a stronger responsibility and hence the necessity of being accountable to stakeholders."

Betten tells me about the mind shift that is taking place in many companies, from *shareholder value* to *stakeholder value,* as it is the case with DSM:

> Not long ago, this accountability (and reporting) was primarily aiming at the shareholder, and listed companies were often the only ones with a (financial) annual report. But a company, whether listed or not, has many more stakeholders than just the ones holding shares. Employees, local residents, customers, suppliers, the government, and societal organizations – they too have an interest in the affairs of an enterprise. When DSM's Board decided in 2010 that we would integrate the financial report and the *Triple P* report, I became very enthusiastic. Of course, in practice it was not always

easy, but thanks to the hard work of a large group of colleagues, we were able to join the non-financial issues with the financial ones and to publish one combined report at the start of 2011.

This integrated report was partly based on the directives of the *Global Reporting Initiative* (GRI), an international standard for transparent reporting. In order to show you some aspects of this transparency at DSM, I selected a few quotes from the annual report. I don't use the two award-winning editions of 2011 and 2012, but the third integrated report of 2013, which has been further improved.

"As part of its 2010–2015 strategy, DSM in motion: driving focused growth, the company has taken sustainability to the next level. In addition to fulfilling its own responsibilities toward society, DSM has successfully developed sustainability as a strategic driver of growth. (. . .)"

As part of the strengthening of the regional associations, DSM established a regional China Sustainability Committee in 2012, which helps to create more awareness of sustainability as a business driver at DSM China. DSM initiated the China *Triple P* Supplier Engagement and Development project in July 2013, in partnership with Solidaridad and Manpower. The aim is to use the people, planet, and profit angle to engage suppliers to create a more sustainable supply chain.

DSM India has defined a sustainability roadmap with specific focus areas, and these are being driven by an India Sustainability platform comprised of the different business groups led by the DSM India president.

In August, *Feed & Food* magazine (Brazil) awarded DSM a *Troféu Curuca de Sustentabilidade*, the Brazilian 'sustainability Oscar for agribusiness.' The award was given in recognition of the technologies and solutions DSM has developed in the fight against hunger around the globe, as published in the article "Vitamins for Human Development" in the 68th edition of the magazine."

There are many more remarkable texts in the annual report of 2013 that I would love to show you – for example, the one about the *People LCA* tool. It is the *people* equivalent of the *planet*-oriented LCA method – the *lifecycle assessment* – that allows you to calculate the environmental impact a product has, and which many companies have applied for years. Then there is the part about research toward developing a system of social standards for sustainable and innovative procurement in Europe and Asia, in which the occurring social issues are considered realistically through the eyes of stakeholders. Another text deals with the *Global Suppliers Sustainability Program*, through which DSM actively encourages its supplier to operate and produce sustainably. But I will hold back and not go on about sustainability at DSM; after all, you can download their annual reports yourself and study them. (For the web link, see the last pages of the book.)

The reports don't just mention the positive stories. As the jury of the Crystal Award explains appreciatively, the report is open and honest about 'what still went wrong.' Two such incidents happened in 2012: "At DSM Sinochem Pharmaceuticals in Yushu (China), a dust explosion occurred in the packing area of the site. Fortunately, there were no injuries, but this incident has been classified as a serious near miss. At DSM Ahead in the Netherlands, an employee had his work restricted because his skin became irritated by the substances he had been working with."

Regarding the company strategy and transparency, DSM is involved in a continuing dialogue with all kinds of stakeholders. Besides shareholders, customers, and employees, the report also mentions suppliers, local communities, end users, comparable companies, financial institutions, governments, investors, NGOs, and interest groups.

Still, in spite of two Crystal Awards, Herman Betten is not yet satisfied. He has new plans, as he writes to me: "It is nearly the time to start the preparations for the fourth integrated report. Again, there is the challenge to raise the bar further concerning the contents, the clarity, and the transparency, for being accountable automatically implies being transparent.

The next step toward transparency is clear: The Environmental Profit & Loss, i.e. a calculation in which not just the immediate costs are included but also the indirect costs for mankind and the environment. It is a logical next step as adding value and being transparent not only relates to financial issues."

THE ACHIEVEMENT

You are personally accountable with respect to society.

This means:

- *You describe your professional activities, their goals and outcomes, and the consequences for all possible stakeholders openly and honestly, in a way that is clearly understandable to all stakeholders.*
- *You do this for the benefit of your immediate colleagues and your executives. Besides, you do it for the benefit of all kinds of others who are involved or interested. Think of your partner, your children, your parents, your neighbors, reporters, public servants, interest groups, citizens, or schools. For each of them, you select a suitable and appealing way of communicating.*
- *If it concerns formal reporting, you apply recognized standards for transparency as a minimum criterion, and you work continuously on the improvement of the reporting.*

Being held accountable can take the shape of formal reports or of presentations, articles, or books. Besides, there are other less formal means for accounting, for example, through conversations, public discussions, stories, columns, websites, blogs, tweets, online forums, and TV programs.

Accountability is not only about the entire company formally being held accountable, as reported by specialized employees. Accountability is also related to each individual professional, both inside and outside of the company he or she works for. That is why your partner, your children, or your parents, etc. were mentioned.

For the transparency of annual reports, the standards of the Crystal Award offer a valid hold. On the website of the Crystal, the criteria for the transparency benchmark can be downloaded. Some of them are:

Issue 2.2

Does the accounting information offer an explanation about the impact of the own operations on people, the environment, and society?

> *Explanation: 'impact' implies the main consequences (effects on e.g. stakeholders) of the core processes and activities of the organization related to sustainable development (e.g. CO_2 emissions, industrial accidents, waste disposal, et cetera).*

- *No (0 points)*
- *Yes (2 points)*

Issue 8.2

Which of the issues below does the explanation concerning chain responsibility discuss?

Check those issues and indicate where these discussions are to be found in the accountability information:

- *Human rights, and the strategic principles and goals the organization applies on this issue. (+1 point)*
- *Bribery and corruption, and the strategic principles and goals the organization applies on this issue. (+1 point)*
- *The extent of the policy concerning suppliers, by explaining to which extent demands are posed upon indirect suppliers. (+1 point)*
- *The explanation does not go into the above issues. (0 points)*

Issue 13.1

Does the accountability information contain an explanation about the way in which the dialogue with stakeholders is structured?

- *No (0 points)*
- *Yes (2 points)*

Issue 13.2
Does the accountability information offer feedback from the stakeholders themselves?

- *No (0 points)*
- *Yes (+2 points)*

Other important norms and guiding lines for transparency are to be found in the already mentioned *Global Reporting Initiative* (GRI), in ISO 26000, and in the *Dow Jones Sustainability Index* (DJSI). Some of the top-ranking companies in 2014 on the DJSI are: Siemens (Germany, category: Capital Goods), Abbott Laboratories (the United States, category: Healthcare Equipment & Services), Unilever (the Netherlands, category: Food, Beverage & Tobacco), Wipro Ltd (India, category: Software & Services), and LG Electronics (the Republic of Korea, category: Consumer Durables & Apparel).

CHAPTER THREE
Competent professionals

A competence: What is it, really? Or, to put it another way, what is a competent professional? Quite a few books have been written about these two questions using highly complex theories – now and then based on thorough scientific studies. But it does not have to be that difficult. Actually, it is very simple:

> *A competent professional is someone you will ask to do a job for you again.*

This is because he or she recently did it in a way you liked.

THE COMPETENT PLUMBER

In order to imagine how someone like that would act, I thought to myself, let me not start in a way that's too complicated. No abstract kind of profession that I cannot grasp easily. Instead, I will look at a professional who has a clearly visible task in an environment I know well.

So, as a starting point, I imagined a dramatic situation in my own house. A small catastrophe, an imaginary situation, by the way, not a real one, thank goodness. What has happened? My son, three years old, has – just for fun – been hanging on the bathroom sink, which has completely broken off the wall and is now lying on the floor. My son is all right, but the bathroom less so. The water pipe has shattered into pieces, and now I have a beautiful "fountain" right where I always dreamed of *not* having one. Water is gushing out! It has already flooded the bathroom floor and the landing and is starting to run down my stairs like a waterfall. My hall and living room are about to turn into a sea. What about me – what do I do? I can think of just one thing to do: panic!

"Call the plumber . . ." I sigh, and so I do. Later, the plumber arrives. So now, what do you expect he – our plumber is a male – will do, as a competent professional?

The first thing he does is eliminate the immediate cause of my problem, making sure that it does not get any worse. That is to say, he needs to find the main water supply line and turn the shut-off valve handle. And he definitely should not ask me where this handle is, for I am panicking right now. All of a sudden, I don't know anything anymore. So, the good man has to know, all on his own, where he has the biggest chance of finding the shut-off valve: in this case, downstairs under the doormat by my front door. Without hesitation, he lifts the mat, removes the wooden panel, and shuts off the main water line. Well, that's something.

The second thing he does is calm me down so that I can contribute something useful. So he starts talking to me, telling me things like: "Look, it isn't really so bad. It's clean water after all. We will fix it. Now, if you could get me a couple of buckets and some towels, I will . . ." et cetera. It is reassuring when he does that. My mind clears a little, and my sense returns.

Only after this has been done, the plumber will go upstairs, equipped with the necessary tools, where he will start doing the things you would expect primarily from a person like him. So he will "plumb," or whatever it may accurately be called, and start repairing the water pipe and the sink.

WHAT HE ACTUALLY DID

Look, someone who acts in such a calm, competent way is definitely a professional. And, he did much more than just the technical stuff you might associate first when you think of his profession. In his first act in this terrible situation, his role was primarily that of a disaster fighter. His action, his achievement, was to shut off the main water line. In doing this, he made use of his architectural insight regarding how houses in my country are usually constructed. At that moment, the tool he used was his architectural insight. In his second achievement, calming me down and giving me some directions, he acted in a very different role, that of an aid worker. The tool he used this time was his knowledge of people.

Only in his third role, he performed as a technician when he started repairing. For this, I guess, he used tools such as pipe wrenches and a soldering torch.

CONTEXT, ROLES, ACHIEVEMENTS, AND TOOLS

*C*ontext, roles, achievement, and tools – these together define competences. I will give you a brief overview.

Context:
Inundation in my bathroom

Role #1:
Disaster fighter
Achievement:
Find main water line and turn it off
Tool:
Architectural insight

Role #2:
Aid worker
Achievement:
Calm people down, give directions
Tool:
Knowledge of people

Role #3:
Technician
Achievement:
Repair broken sink
Tools:
Pipe wrenches, soldering torch, etc.

In my catastrophe scenario, the plumber established three different competences, and at the right moment, he shifted fluently from one role to another. This wonderful example – it is *almost* a shame it did not really happen – provides answers for the two questions this chapter started with.

> A **competence** is the ability to deliver, in a given **context**, in a certain **role**, solid **achievements** by making use of appropriate **tools**.

> A **competent professional** is someone who is able, in a range of contexts, to shift flexibly between the various roles that are demanded, and who delivers solid achievements in each of them.

A person who has proved being able to do that – that's someone you will ask to do a job for you again.

What about you? In what kind of context do you usually work, and which roles are demanded from you there? Have you ever been a disaster fighter, an aid worker, a technician, or something else? Which tools to you possess? And above all which achievement are you proud of?

CHAPTER FOUR

Emotional intelligence

The Competence (Figure 4.1):

A sustainably competent professional empathizes with the values and emotions of others.

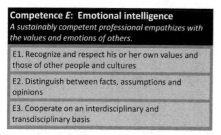

Figure 4.1 *Competence E: Emotional Intelligence*

"I am a good listener." This is one of the items in an EQ test you can find on the Internet. You may be familiar with the EQ, the emotional intelligence quotient, meant to complement the IQ: emotions versus intelligence. "I understand how other people feel," is an item from another EQ test. This chapter focuses on these types of themes.

Whereas the competence of Chapter 2, responsibility, deals with the relationship between the professional and his or her tasks and is therefore *task-oriented* or *case-focused*, Chapter 3 explores the relationship between the professional and other individuals and groups and is consequently *people-oriented*. The ability to relate on an emotional level to others strongly depends on whether you recognize and empathize with the values and norms of that person, and whether you are able to compare them to your own.

This chapter, too, brings you three concrete achievements that you can accomplish as a professional. This time they are:

- *Recognize and respect your own values and those of other people and cultures*
- *Distinguish between facts, assumptions, and opinions*
- *Cooperate beyond the limits of your own discipline*

4.1 RESPECT VALUES OF YOURSELF AND OTHERS

Our student body is 17% Hispanic/Latino, 82% African-American, 1% Asian/Mixed Race. A large number of our students were incarcerated, experienced violence, grieved the death of a relative or friend, endured an unsafe passage into the US, and/or still live within other ills of society.

This is the beginning of a story told by Genevieve Maignan-Keogh, a school counselor who was born in Haiti and grew up in Algeria, Morocco, Libya, Italy, and the United States. She works at an inner-city high school in Washington, D.C. Genevieve continues:

"Two months into the 2013–14 school year, students and parents alike, expressed concern about one of our instructors, Mr. Bendjedid (not his real name). They accused him of being confrontational and demeaning and had a difficult time understanding his accent. A student said, 'if you ask him a question, he'll say: Why don't you understand? It makes us feel like we should know as soon as he explains.' At first I thought the students were rebelling, as do many teens. This was my first year at this school; I was unfamiliar with the teacher's practices. I met him the first week of school and detected a strong accent as he shared great stories of his many travels, his published work, people he knew, students he helped, etc. He was definitely a confident guy. I did find him collegial. We had quite a bit in common; he was Algerian, spoke five languages, and had lived in some of the same countries I had lived in."

"The student complaints arrived almost in concert with Mr. Bendjedid's request to remove certain students from his English class," Genevieve explains. "As the calls and emails came in from angry parents and students, I realized that the issue was bigger than what I had thought! I organized one meeting at a time and invited the parent(s), student, and teacher to address their concerns. I had it all planned out. I would give everyone a chance to express their point of view, process what was being said, and propose strategies that would help the student succeed."

"There were times when I met with Mr. Bendjedid outside of parent meetings. He often looked frustrated and a couple of times said, 'How am I supposed to teach them? This student doesn't speak English well and can't write. Other students barely passed English 1, are reading at the 2nd grade level, and are in my class. You're setting me up for failure.' Mr. Bendjedid also believed that the students were not interested in learning, did not try to improve, and did not participate. During one of our meetings, I told him that the student was a Level 3 English Language Learner and thus needed to be mainstreamed. I also reminded him that I could not retain students who passed the class. I remember feeling cornered; I felt as though Mr. Benjedid was talking at me, rather than *with* me. I looked down at the list of names he wanted removed from his class when he suddenly exclaimed: 'Look at me when I'm talking to you!' I looked around to see who he was talking to, but there was no one else; he was speaking to me!"

"I guess he thought I was being disrespectful, or I was not paying attention to him," recalls Genevieve. "However, when I was growing up, eye contact signified disrespect, especially when adults reprimanded you or accused you of something. In American culture, it is the opposite. I have assimilated to American culture, but looking away still comes naturally for me. I've tried to change this, but it's difficult."

Although it might have been easier to condemn Mr. Benjedid, Genevieve decided to explore the triggers that created discomfort at the meetings and realized that cultural nuances played a role in their relationship. His education was more structured, one-sided, and didactic than that of present public education. She knew this from her own experience as a student in the French system. Although they had similar experiences, Genevieve recognized that she would have to respect the teacher's cultural uniqueness and perception.

Genevieve elaborates, "Approaching student-teacher conflict is a sensitive issue. I am primarily there to advocate for the student, but I am also obligated to uphold a professional relationship with colleagues. I felt this could only be attained by allowing everyone to speak their truth, respecting the student and the teacher, by remaining impartial, and most importantly, by reminding those present that my purpose is to advocate for the student. It took me over a year to realize that our cultural similarities were in conflict. Individual perception exacerbated the conflict. I was forced to revisit my cultural norms, which were formed during my primary years, and accepted that my personal experiences clouded how I interpreted the teacher's actions.

When I lived and attended school in North Africa, teachers were always right. Corporal punishment was a common practice. Fear of the adult meant respect. In addition, I lived in countries where men criticized, demeaned, and oppressed women. Mr. Benjedid's approach reminded me of that fear and oppression. Subconsciously, I was resisting colluding with his notion that children's opinions and feelings did not matter. I did not want to engage in ridiculing children's rights. I was also rejecting what I interpreted to be gender-bias and prejudicial attacks."

It was difficult for Genevieve to keep her feelings in check, but she managed by being as objective as possible. "Every time I felt attacked, my instinct was to go into survival mode. I needed to defend the students, and myself. With each instance, I fought my primordial need to save face, and removed the feelings from the situation. I guess this relationship was the tipping point, which forced me to take a step back. I had to ask myself, 'What is the perceived threat?' and 'Where is this feeling coming from?' These two questions help me navigate through other conflicts, which also derive from cultural differences."

And how did this particular conflict with Mr. Benjedid get solved you may wonder? According to Genevieve, the complaints from students, parents, and the teacher continued, and neither party was able to rise above its subjective perspective. She concludes, "The principal eventually merged two social studies classes, in order to free up a teacher, and created a new section of English 2. Mr. Benjedid gave me a list of students he wanted removed, and I enrolled them in the new English 2 section."

Looking back, Genevieve feels that this challenging experience strengthened her abilities to navigate through cultural intricacies. "Respect, introspection, and the will to change – those are three important skills necessary to go beyond misleading interpretations and move toward solutions. I always start with respect because that is what keeps us civilized. For me, respect means understanding that all lives have a purpose and matter. It means recognizing that there are differences, and not necessarily understanding why those differences exist. Introspection is next because that is where change begins. The will to change follows because it takes courage. Ultimately, the only one you can change is yourself."

THE ACHIEVEMENT

You recognize and respect values, both your own and those of other people and cultures.

This means:

- *You formulate the values from which you think and act as a professional.*
- *You do the same for or with others who are involved or have an interest in your professional actions.*
- *In order to do that, you "listen actively" to others, and you communicate with them respectfully about the differences in values. Whatever you say or write about them, you check with them.*
- *When you cooperate with others, you utilize both the similarities and differences of values as an enrichment and reinforcement of the quality of your activities.*

Actively listening is much more than just hearing what the other says. It is trying to understand what is *being* said, and what is *not* being said but intended. It means ask further if you don't understand the things the other person is trying to say, and it means that you check whether you have understood the other person correctly, for instance, by repeating or summarizing the message in your own words.

Actively listening also implies that you let the other person realize that you are listening and that you are interested in what they have to say. You signal this not only with words (verbally) but also through your posture and gestures (non-verbally).

Concerning values, relevant concepts include cultural values, ethical norms, beliefs, religion, philosophy of life, and traditions. The above story about Genevieve Maignan-Keogh's work deals with personal values, cultural sensitivity, and mutual respect.

Reader, I have a confession to make. In the first years after I started working for sustainable development in 1991, I rarely thought about these human aspects of sustainability. In those days, I primarily discussed the importance of science and technology. I thought if we were able to close the cycles of products and materials (what we now call C2C, "Cradle to Cradle"), calculate the environmental impact of our products and processes with the aid of life cycle assessment (see Chapter 2) to minimize the impact, and use sustainable sources of energy, then the world would become sustainable. Perhaps you will forgive my naïveté when I tell you that I graduated in theoretical physics and that in those years, I was the manager of a brand-new education program called "sustainable technology," which was partly designed by me. No wonder I was biased. My personal management education had only just begun, let alone my Ph.D. program in social sciences, which I completed between 2006 and 2010.

In the 25 years between then and now, my view on sustainable development has shifted fundamentally. The fact that I am at present – following famous scientists and authors – writing about a balance between people, planet, and profit is a consequence of a personal transition over the course of the first ten of those 25 years: from mainly *planet* to the entire *Triple P*.

It's funny. My co-author, Prof. Rachelson, tells me that for her dissertation she researched the attitudes, beliefs, and practices of community college professors regarding sustainable development. She interviewed professors about their personal journeys toward sustainability, their definitions and interpretations of what sustainability entails, and their ideas for infusing sustainability into the higher education curriculum.

If I think about which topic currently touches me most deeply, it is certainly *people*. Sure, planet issues are incredibly important. If we don't find ways to solve the climate crisis or fail to sufficiently protect the tropical forest and biodiversity, we are heading toward global catastrophes. The profit themes are also of crucial importance because as long as we don't succeed in designing a system in which the world economy becomes more stable and in which sustainable energy, food, and industrial products become more financially attractive, the world will never be sufficiently sustainable. All this is true. But when I see how people like Genevieve advocate for their disadvantaged students, I am deeply touched. It also moves me when I read how homosexuals are granted the legal right to marry, women and minorities the right to vote and to acquire leadership positions in business and society, children the right to safety, health, and education, religious and non-religious people the right to freedom of speech, and the elderly the right to a dignified and self-decided end of life. This is all about human dignity, to which everybody is entitled, about respect, and finally about everyone's right to be considered as a person, to exercise self-expression, and to participate actively in society. These are the highest goals of sustainable development in my view: emancipation, empowerment, participation, cultural diversity, and personal and social identity. It short, it is about the right to be who you are.

These kinds of topics concern each and every professional. *Environmental, technological,* or *economic* sustainability may primarily be topics for specialists. In Chapter 11, which deals with different kinds of specialists, you will find some nice examples of them, but every professional in each and every discipline can strengthen *human* sustainability. The next story sets another great example.

4.2 FACTS, ASSUMPTIONS, AND OPINIONS

Phew! I get really tired when Sandra Veenstra tells me about her clients. Sandra is a psychotherapist who treats all kinds of problems her patients complain about, often a combination of medical and psychological issues. One of these patients was Mrs. H., whom Sandra had diagnosed as chronically fatigued. According to the patient, Mrs. H. herself was not blame. She was sure about that, she told Sandra.

However, when the psychotherapist inquired what Mrs. H. did on an average day, the patient produced a long list. In the morning, she took her children to school and picked them up afterwards. She did the family's grocery shopping, cared for the disabled aunt, cleaned the windows (inside and outside), vacuumed the house daily, ironed clothes, dusted the furniture, changed the bed sheets at least once a week, and much, much more. Quite a lot of work for a chronically fatigued patient!

The situation was rather serious. Mrs. H. had quit her part-time job. Not only did she suffer but so did her husband, son, and daughter. Mrs. H. was often depressed, yelled at her children, and lashed out at her husband, who could not take it anymore. The family was about to fall apart.

A typical case for cognitive behavioral therapy, the psychologist decided. This type of therapy implies that you start investigating whether the patient's ideas, her *cognitions*, are based upon facts or not, and what the implications for her behavior are.

"Why do you clean your windows every week?" Sandra inquired.

"Well, that's what should be done, right? I've learned it that way!" the patient replied, visibly proud.

"Aha," said Sandra. "The same is true for vacuuming the house every day, I suppose?"

"Certainly. This is what a good homemaker should do," Mrs. H. answered.

Ah, a typical example of a "should-ism." Another one quickly followed:

"And what about your aunt, do you really have to take care of her?" Sandra asked.

"Of course, I should," was the answer. "My aunt is seriously ill. She can't do that herself!"

Sandra continued with the interview, trying to discover together with her patient if all those "certainties" were really that certain. What would happen if she cleaned the windows less frequently? Would the house collapse? Would people start to think badly about her? Step by step, Sandra challenged her patient's cognitions. All should-isms were exposed, one by one. Were they really facts or opinions?

"Suppose you would vacuum the house less than once a day," Sandra asked Mrs. H. "What exactly could go wrong?"

"Well, I . . . I'm not sure, but . . . I would certainly feel uncomfortable!"

It took a while before Mrs. H. acknowledged that the necessity of vacuuming every day was an opinion and not a proven fact. On the other hand, it became clear that her aunt was seriously disabled and did need help. No doubt about that.

"But, is it really *you* who has to offer all the help? Aren't there any other family members who can contribute?" Sandra wanted to know.

"Ha, they will never do that, I'm sure!" Mrs. H. asserted.

"Are you sure?" asked Sandra.

"Oh yeah, meet my family!" Mrs. H. replied.

Was this a fact, as Mrs. H. stated, or was it an assumption?

Sandra asked, "Have you ever asked them?"

"No. No reason. I just know what they are going to say," was Mrs. H's response.

Right, it was an assumption. Following Sandra's advice, Mrs. H. started to reevaluate, and within a month, the family came to an agreement about taking turns caring for the disabled aunt.

Over the course of a series of therapy sessions, the patient discovered that there are many tasks that are not really necessary and that it is one's own choice how frequently one does laundry, dusts, or cleans. Mrs. H. decided to change the bed sheets once a month and to vacuum the living room once a week. As she spent the time she gained on relaxing and recovering, her constant strain ended, and she found a healthy balance. Her condition improved, and after a few months, she concluded that "actually, she was not chronically fatigued" anymore. Her mood improved, her energy increased, and she finally found the time to dedicate her attention to her family and hobbies. Mrs. H's entire family recuperated considerably, and her marriage was saved.

THE ACHIEVEMENT

You distinguish between facts, assumptions, and opinions.

This means:

- *When it comes to assertions (both your own and those of others), you determine whether they are facts, assumptions, or opinions.*

- *You communicate your conclusions in such a way that others, including the person who made the assertion, come to a consensus.*
- *During your professional activities, you decide when a fact, an assumption, or an opinion is needed, and you plan accordingly.*
- *Whenever necessary, you design acceptable and realistic methods to turn an opinion or an assumption into a fact, or to replace a fact with an assumption and/or an opinion.*

Facts, assumptions, and opinions – these often get mixed up. Moreover, and perhaps equally catastrophic, not everyone is always aware when hard facts are required and when insisting on them may be less wise. Let me give you an example.

Every now and then, the following happens: a village or town gets agitated over a certain local hazard – let's say, over radiation coming from a recently installed cellphone tower. People have noticed, let me assume, that a significant number of leukemia cases have been diagnosed in the nearby area. They are absolutely sure that this is due to the cellphone tower. "That damn cellphone tower has to go!" people demand. Fair or unfair?

Policymakers and politicians know that this issue is a hornet's nest because all kinds of assertions intersect: facts, assumptions, and opinions. For instance: "A significant number of leukemia cases have been diagnosed." This assertion may be a fact. If so, it is an outcome of thorough scientific research, in which the number of leukemia cases has been exactly determined and compared to a control group, corrected for variables such as age structure, educational level, socio-economic status, ethnic background, presence of highways and industrial areas, and at least 20 other factors that might influence the statistics.

Next, the researchers have determined that – yes, indeed – the percentage of leukemia patients is to a statistically significant extent higher than might be expected. After a scrupulous review by "peers," i.e. by other scientific researchers who are relevant experts, they publish the results in an international medical journal. In short, this hypothesis is *evidence-based*. By the way, even then it may happen that additional scientific research establishes that the so-called "fact" appears doubtful.

However, it is just as likely that the "significantly higher number of leukemia patients" is only an assumption that resulted from the fact that, by coincidence, two children suffering from leukemia live in the same street, which got the rumor mill working.

The next remark – "That damn cellphone tower has to go!" – most certainly is an opinion and not a fact. What can you do in such a situation if you are the one who is professionally responsible for it? Set up genuine scientific research? Perhaps, if you have the opinion that the outcome will help – and that it will be published in time. However, real life has shown that scientific facts rarely help in a situation like this. Mostly opinions and emotions count, and usually they don't change when facts contradicting the general opinions are offered.

The example above illustrates how important it is to decide what is needed – in every context – facts, assumptions, or opinions. It also illustrates the possibility of flexibly changing from one to the other, for instance, by turning an assumption into a fact based on solid investigation. The example also demonstrates the limits of such a change in real-life situations.

Taking the (more or less) reverse approach can also yield results. Instead of striving for objectivity, you can start a quest for *intersubjectivity*, i.e. for generally shared and supported assumptions or opinions. You may find that scientific proof, showing that the cellphone tower cannot possibly cause leukemia, causes anger and aggression. If so, it will probably be wiser not to rely on this evidence. Instead, you might focus on the emotions to find out if the community can come to a consensus about what should happen: remove the cell tower even if no scientific evidence supports it, or not?

4.3 COOPERATION

There is an ascending series of words: *monodisciplinary – multidisciplinary – interdisciplinary – transdisciplinary.*

I immediately want to add that not everyone uses these four words in the same way. I will just tell you how I use them, in accordance with how (as far as I have observed it) they are most generally used.

If a teacher of physics – as I myself have been for quite a few years – designs a lesson just on his own, focusing solely on the physics content of the lesson, he is working in a *monodisciplinary* style, completely within the boundaries of his own discipline. If he prepares a thematic week about nature and the environment – still on his own – he is working *multidisciplinarily* at that moment: in his head, he combines elements from a variety of disciplines.

Maybe such preparation will result in a magnificent thematic week, but it is to be expected that this week will become much more wonderful and enriched when the teacher of physics cooperates with colleagues from different disciplines, and maybe even with the school psychologist, the career counselor, the janitor, and a bunch of external experts. This cooperation of a variety of experts is called *interdisciplinary*, literally: "between the disciplines."

But it can be even better. Many aspects of nature and the environment can be discussed, and not just by experts. You may include "ordinary" people: inhabitants of the region, representatives of action groups, walkers, and cyclists. They are all persons who feel connected to the topic of the thematic week, not because they are experts in a relevant discipline but for other reasons. When you also actively involve these stakeholders in the preparation of the thematic week, you make them members of a *transdisciplinary* team, literally a team "beyond the disciplines."

In short:

Monodisciplinary = one or more experts, one discipline
Multidisciplinary = one expert, several disciplines
Interdisciplinary = several experts in cooperation, each from his/her own discipline
Transdisciplinary = interdisciplinary + stakeholders without some special expertise

The crowdsourcing project involving Simone Lopulisa and her bank that Chapter 2 starts with is a nice example of a transdisciplinary approach. Not only were the bank experts actively involved in the stakeholder analysis, all kinds of people and societal organizations were also invited to join in, and it proved to be successful.

Here is another successful story – about "Transition Towns."

The American Wikipedia entry describes a transition town as:

> *A grassroots community project that seeks to build resilience in response to peak oil, climate destruction, and economic stability by creating local groups that uphold the values of the transition network.*

The Dutch Wikipedia adds to this:

> *Transition Town: a local community (city, quarter or village) that takes the initiative to make its way of living, working and housing more sustainable.*

The Transition Town (TT) movement started in the village of Totnes in England in 2006. From there, the idea quickly spread to 50 countries around the world. According to Transition United States, the nonprofit umbrella organization that supports networking between transition initiatives in the United States, there are currently 163 Transition Towns in 37 states (October 2017). A person who can explain how cooperation in a Transition Town works is Kirk Ritchey, a Transition Town core member and organizer from TT Woodstock, New York.

Woodstock rings a bell? Some of you may have heard the name in a very different context – the 1969 music festival that influenced generations featuring Jimi Hendrix, Joe Cocker, Janis Joplin, Santana, etc. – but these days, the town is making an impact in other ways. In 2012, the community joined a growing number of towns and municipalities worldwide and officially became a Transition Town with the goal of "building local resilience through community action."

A TT initiative is set up by a horizontal network organization and local thematic working groups around themes such as sustainable energy, urban agriculture, local economy, biodiversity, education, and transportation. Volunteers from a variety of professional backgrounds do most of the work in a TT GROUP.

Kirk Ritchey was initially drawn to TT Woodstock because he loves cycling and felt that the town needed safer streets and more bike lanes. His working group – Transportation – advocates for "safe passages and lanes for pedestrians & bicyclists" and also seeks to "increase awareness of safety for pedestrians & bicyclists and the value of vehicle slow zones throughout Woodstock."

In order to act collectively, TT organizers like Ritchey must know how to work with people across different disciplines in a cooperative way. "Transportation," Ritchey says, "is a perfect example. The goal is to establish an incremental improvement plan, so you need to interface with the local government, residents, and other volunteer organizations. To qualify for grants, organizations need to get their projects into the county's official comprehensive plan," explains Ritchey, and to this end, he and other like-minded residents from different Woodstock-based volunteer organizations have formed the Active Transportation Advisory Council "to generate a plan that coordinates with local, county, and state transportation agencies and is adopted by Woodstock's town leaders."

According to Ritchey, "cooperation thrives when you allow people to follow their individual passion, so we started to identify where people's passions lie." In Woodstock, these interdisciplinary passions include garden sharing, wellness, transportation, green energy, and organic waste. "You can't create that," Ritchey emphasizes.

Transition Towns provide people from different backgrounds with opportunities to come together and cooperate. "People seek community; they want to be part of something," Ritchey explains. When people share values, they are more likely to cooperate; however, cooperation is not always easy. "Breakdowns occur. Some people join because of a single interest, for instance, anti-fracking, and this can derail groups from making progress. There are also people who join organizations because they are *against* something. When this happens, you have to go back to the principles and say: Our source of cooperation is based on being *for* something rather than *against* something. Let's stay in touch with what we are *for* and what we share. Adhering to the '7 Guiding Principles of Transition' posted on the group's website is a good starting point."

Ritchey thinks, "Individuals joining the Transition Town movement also have to undergo 'an inner transition.' This includes developing interpersonal skills for group settings." Because people often have difficulty with communication, TT Woodstock created a team called "Working Group Support" to specifically address conflict resolution and help members interact more positively with one another. The group focuses on "strengthening people's relationships, so we were able to avoid dysfunction" Ritchey adds. Wherever they are, Transition Towns are young organizations that rely on forming alliances with other groups. To cooperate, Ritchey says, you "have to work on key relationships, for example, with the fire department, the city council, etc."

Only recently, the town had to mobilize when a water company "set up shop to utilize the town's water," Ritchey remembers. "A lot was at stake. People said, 'Wait a minute. We don't want this going on.' There were a lot of people against the privatization of our local natural resource (water). TT Woodstock provided a forum where people from the community could come together to discuss this issue. We created a platform to look at our watershed from a systemic viewpoint, which we called 'Our watershed is our lifeboat.' Collectively, our town began to understand that it's our responsibility to manage this local resource so it's available to everyone, not just those who will purchase it." The town's efforts worked. The water company eventually withdrew its bid and left Woodstock.

In the meantime, Ritchey's working group – Transportation – continues to generate ideas for better bike lanes, signage, and pedestrian pathways in a cooperative way. They have one year to present their plan to the town's local government and make a positive impact for future generations.

THE ACHIEVEMENT

You act in a multi-, inter-, or even transdisciplinary way.

This means:

- *You act in a multidisciplinary way – In your professional activities you involve aspects of disciplines other than your own.*
- *You act in an interdisciplinary way – You carry out your professional activities as a member of an interdisciplinary team in which you cooperate intensively with professionals from a variety of other disciplines.*
- *You act in a transdisciplinary way – You also actively involve others, who don't represent a specific professional discipline but who have a stake in what you do for other reasons, in your professional activities. This may involve experiential experts but also amateurs or laymen who for whatever reason are or feel included. It may concern individuals but also representatives of groups.*

Transition Towns and transition initiatives – if perhaps you are not fully familiar with the concept of transition, you may appreciate it if I tell you that it is a "fundamental change of a system based upon a paradigm shift." A *paradigm* is a concept that – in just one word – describes a whole way of thinking, and a *paradigm shift* is a fundamental change in the way people think and talk about things. During a transition, not just a physical system changes, but also the underlying notions, values, and ethical norms. An example from the ancient past is the transition from a hunter and gatherer society to one based on agriculture, accompanied by the transition from a nomadic to a sedentary community. More recent transitions are the industrial revolution, the rise of democracy and human rights, the foundation and growth of the United Nations and the European Union, and the introduction of the present IT-based society starting with the telegraph, continuing with the telephone, radio and TV, and presently arriving at computers, automation, the Internet, and smart phones, smart grids, smart houses, and smart cars.

Many global systems have been arranged in a highly unsustainable way. This is true, for example, for the international system of agriculture and food as well as for the energy sector, which is almost completely based on fossil fuels. Not only are we approaching peak oil, but aside from that, oil, gas, and coal are destroying our climate.

Before going to Chapter 6, in which I will tell you more about systems and the next sustainability competence, *systems thinking*, I first want to share a little more about professionals who are not just competent as such, but who are *sustainably* competent. We need a great many of them.

CHAPTER FIVE

Sustainably competent professionals

When I ask people what they associate with the word "sustainability," some will immediately mention nature and the environment: climate change, for instance, or aerosols.

Others will quickly add, "But wait, sustainability, isn't that about people, too?" And when asked for an explanation, they may mention poverty and hunger in developing countries, refugees, or discrimination and issues concerning a multicultural society.

Yes! Sustainable development is about many, many issues. Sometimes this makes it hard for people to understand the concept properly. It may seem as if *every* problem we are struggling with – in the world, in Europe, Africa, or Asia, in our country, or even in our own town or village – has to do with sustainability. Many people have the feeling that "sustainability" is some sort of container into which you can throw each and every problem in the entire world. If this is true, then what's the use of such a word? What does it explain? How can you ever know how to live or work in a sustainable way?

The concept of "sustainable development" was used for the first time in 1980, in a publication of three global organizations for nature and the environment. One of them was the World Wildlife Fund. In the following years, the Brundtland Commission performed a thorough study on behalf of the United Nations. In 1987, the commission published its final report called "Our Common Future." According to the report, sustainable development is:

> *"a development that meets the needs of the present without compromising the ability of future generations to meet their own needs."*

In other words: On the one hand, sustainable development is about now: about the desire to grant every person in the world a decent life. This concerns, for example, combating poverty and hunger. Moreover, it includes quality education and healthcare for everybody – wherever in the world – a healthy living environment, freedom, democracy, safety, and human rights. In short, it gives each human the chance to be a full member of society.

On the other hand, sustainable development is also about later: about the concerns that we are overexploiting our planet with our present lifestyle. It is about our desire to grant our children, grandchildren, and great-grandchildren a decent future, which is only possible if we drastically change our present way of living.

SOLUTIONS THAT REALLY WORK

Yeah, but – some people ask me – are those two, *now* and *later*, really connected? What makes sustainable development different from a grab bag of issues, a *container concept*? Actually, all those issues in the "grab bag" are strongly linked to one another; they influence each other in many ways.

Let me just give you one example. One of the big issues of our generation is world population growth. This growth takes place at dazzling speed. It took mankind hundreds of thousands of years to grow to one billion people. This point was reached around the year 1800. The second billion took us less than 130 years. In 2011, we completed the seventh billion, an accomplishment we achieved in just 12 years!

What is driving such growth? All right, sex, of course. But that is certainly not the only answer. An important key lies in the fact that population growth occurs almost entirely in poor countries. Why there? Because the people there need children to provide for them in old age. When you live in poverty, your children are seen as the only ones who will feed you, clothe you, and house you when you are old. Moreover, if child mortality in your country is high, you may certainly hope to have a lot of kids! It's a fixed pattern: *everywhere where prosperity increases, the birth rate decreases.* In various wealthy countries, the population is shrinking slightly.

If you want your great-grandchildren to have a decent future, global population growth must come to a halt; so much is absolutely certain. If not, our planet will not survive! Managing population growth depends upon solid economic growth in developing countries. So even if you don't wish for poor people to become prosperous out of a feeling of solidarity or compassion, you still would be wise to wish them prosperity from a rational perspective. It is quintessential for your own future and that of your own children and their offspring.

On the other hand, such strong economic growth may, of course, increase the global *ecological footprint* considerably as the present Republic of China illustrates, for example, unless we find clever ways to avoid this. Partly, this can be done with the help of new science and technology. The rest will have to be accomplished through changes in our behavior as consumers.

This example shows that poverty, economy, ecology, science, technology, and human behavior interact strongly with each other. For that reason, sustainability is not simply a container or grab bag with all problems thrown separately into it. On the contrary, sustainability is the only way to understand the ways in which all those problems and issues are linked and to find solutions that really work.

THE *TRIPLE P*

The way in which the Brundtland Commission describes sustainable development has been generally accepted. However, to be honest, in real life it is hard to apply practically. "*Meet the needs of the present generation.*" Right, but how? And by the way: *which* needs? Everybody drives a second car and gets a new smartphone every six months? "*Future generations*" – wonderful, but how many generations? A thousand?

Many models have been designed to explain sustainability more concretely. One of the best known was created by Ismail Serageldin in

1996: the "*Triple P*," i.e. the three P's: "people," "planet," and "profit." Together they are called the "pillars of sustainability." You have seen them a few times in earlier chapters. Let me summarize:

Social sustainability ("people") at an individual level is about respect for human rights, freedom and safety, cultural values, education and health, personal development, diversity, empowerment, and participation. At a societal level, it concerns peace, democracy, solidarity, and social cohesion.

Ecological sustainability ("planet") relates to conservation and resilience of the natural environment. This implies that ecosystems and biodiversity are protected and that the ability of the natural environment to provide us with resources and regenerate our waste is not harmed.

Economic sustainability ("profit") is present if development toward social and ecological sustainability can take place in a sufficiently stable economic environment and is financially feasible, and if individuals, families, and communities are guaranteed to be free of poverty. (Sometimes, instead of "profit," the broader concept of "prosperity" is used).

Sustainable development means that all aspects and themes above are seen as mutually dependent and interrelated, in that the various interests, problems, and solutions are constantly and harmoniously weighed against and connected with each other. This principle is often: "The three P's must be in balance."

THE NECESSITY OF SUSTAINABLY COMPETENT PROFESSIONALS

The Brundtland report and the *Triple P* don't guarantee that sustainable development is now crystal clear to everybody or that it is easy to decide in all cases, which decisions or actions are sustainable and which are not. Choices concerning sustainable development are usually far from simple. If the use of oil and gas contributes to the greenhouse effect and hence to climate disruption, would it be wise to use nuclear power for a couple of generations, or would that be even more unsustainable? Should we make cars more sustainable, or would that be highly unsustainable in the long term because we might have to get rid of all or most cars? Should we ban child labor in Asia and Africa as fast as we can, even if this means that the parents who depend on their children's income would starve?

No, easy answers don't exist. The dilemmas are complicated, and so are the solutions. At the same time, there are lots of opportunities – opportunities to make the world more beautiful and just than it is at present. Wouldn't it be great if there were no more hunger anywhere? If war could disappear altogether? If all people could live freely and securely? If nature were resilient? I believe these ideas are possible. Whether I am right, I cannot know for sure, but there are two things I do know for sure.

The first certainty is that *if we all believe that the human world is doomed to perish, we will be right*. Negative thinking will become a *self-fulfilling prophecy*, a prediction that makes itself come true, simply because everybody will lean back and do nothing. Consequently, what we should do is roll up our sleeves. Let's work on sustainability with everything we've got!

The second certainty is that *because solutions are complicated, we need everybody to make them work*. Look, at present, a number of companies – large ones and small ones – are contributing intensively to sustainable development, mainly because, by coincidence, they are managed by people who have decided to do so. The same is true for governments of countries. Some have a sustainability policy, but only until the next election brings in another government. In other words, whether a company or a country strives to operate sustainably depends on who happens to be in the executive position, i.e. ultimately by coincidence.

However, sustainable development is far too essential to leave it up to chance. In order for it to become institutionalized, we need everybody, each professional, in lower and higher positions, in whatever enterprise, government, educational institution, or societal organization. We need you, too.

Are you ready?

CHAPTER SIX

Systems orientation

The Competence (Figure 6.1):

A sustainably competent professional thinks and acts from a systemic perspective.

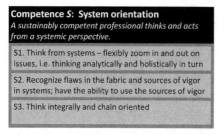

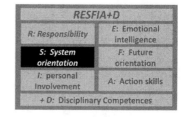

Figure 6.1 *Competence S: Systems orientation*

According to Brundtland, sustainability is about two things. It is about the needs of the people who are living *now*, i.e. about spreading prosperity across the entire planet, and about the needs of the people living *later*. Those two sides of sustainability are often referred to as two *dimensions*: "place" and "time." In Chapter 2, you already encountered the two when they were introduced in the context of responsibility: the consequence scope (= place) and the consequence period (= time).

Competence S, *systems orientation*, is about one of these dimensions: place. This is the topic of the present chapter. The next competence, to be discussed in Chapter 8, is F, *future orientation*. The word already shows that it is the complement of competence S, as it deals with the other dimension: time.

The systems we humans have built across the millennia have not been planned or designed beforehand. They have grown more or less by coincidence, as a kind of evolutionary process. It is not surprising that, in the course of time, many faults and errors have slipped into those systems; they are not just small or insignificant errors, but fundamental weaving faults that are deeply embedded. They are the main causes of unsustainability in our world. The extremely unequal distribution of wealth is one such weaving fault. The instability of the global financial system is another one, causing stock exchange markets to collapse once every few decades with deep economic crises as consequences. The 2008 banking crisis, unfortunately, is a recent example. A third example of a weaving fault is the fact that many loops of our production and consumption of goods are not closed, causing scarcity and depletion of resources on the one hand and mountains of waste and clouds of greenhouse gases on the other.

Not every professional needs to be involved in combating the huge global system errors. Weaving faults exist on every scale and in many systems, in and around companies and their branches, communities and cities, households, and families.

Fortunately, we possess a wide range of sources of vigor against these weaving faults with which we can attack them. Such sources of vigor for sustainability are, for instance, the thousands of local, national, and international organizations such as the Carter Center, UNICEF, and Human Rights Watch. Nature is a source of vigor. Visions, texts, and books can be sources of vigor, sources that inspire people to accomplish grand achievements. Science and technology offer tremendous sources of vigor, just as quite a few companies do. And people, of course. Individual people, and not just in the form of responsible and leading civilians. Every sustainably competent professional is a source of vigor for sustainable development. Each of the heroes in this book is one of them. You are one of them, too.

Below are the three concrete achievements of this chapter:

- *Think from systems: flexibly zoom in and out of issues, i.e. think analytically and holistically in turn*
- *Recognize flaws in the fabric and sources of vigor in systems; utilize the sources of vigor*
- *Think integrally and chain-oriented*

6.1 PARTS AND WHOLES

Let a hundred flowers bloom,

Let a hundred schools of thought contend.

Anonymous, ca. 600 to 221 BC;
often attributed to Mao Zedong, 1956

Sometimes you come across ideas, action groups, or movements, but you are not sure what they actually mean. Do they have a brilliant idea or an intelligent plan offering hope for a sustainable future? Or is it only a nice, romantic but naïve ideal that will never have a significant impact? To me, permaculture is an example of such a doubtful case. I am not yet convinced – time will tell.

Exactly because of this doubt, I think it is great that permaculture exists because sustainable development is not just a matter of neat programs that have already been scientifically tested and validated. That too, of course, but primarily sustainable development is an adventure, a voyage of discovery, in which many exciting new possibilities will be explored. Perhaps many of them will lead to little or nothing, but some of them will prosper and positively conquer the world. That is the thought behind the beautiful ancient Chinese poem about the hundred flowers this section starts with, and the fact that the poem was used or abused by the Chinese party leader Mao Zedong does not alter the case. We live in a magnificent and exciting story.

The Chinese quote fits in two ways with permaculture as it is about flowers and about much more. The practice of permaculture has gained popularity, and its proponents are convinced that it will become even more widely spread. As I said, I don't know yet how smart permaculture is, but Andrew Millison certainly is smart: he studied horticultural conservation at Prescott College, traveled to Cuba to learn about the Cuban people's approaches to organic agriculture, designs permaculture projects, serves as a permaculture consultant, and teaches horticulture at Oregon State University.

If you Google "permaculture" and "the United States," you will find hundreds of places where it is applied. If you simply search "permaculture," you will find thousands.

According to Andrew Millison, "Permaculture has spread a lot in the US, especially in the last few years. There was a time that demonstration sites were found mostly at urban and suburban scales. In part this was because the social environment of permaculture courses was more alternative, and this limited the types of people interested. But with the rise of online courses and a much broader range of media, a wider range of people are adopting permaculture design and methodology. There's literally an explosion of interest in this country, at rural, suburban and urban scales."

Reflecting on the state of permaculture in the United States, Millison adds, "Organizationally, it's more chaotic in the US than in other countries. Places like the UK have a very organized network of students, teachers and practitioners. The US is so geographically dispersed and polarized politically, that there are many different permaculture organizations and groups that are not collaborative with each other. It's a bit of the 'Wild West' out there in the US Permaculture field. This leads to a lot of competition and innovation, for better and for worse."

When Andrew Millison receives a phone call from a potential client, the first thing he usually asks is: "What's your address?" Of course, Millison needs to find out where he will later meet the client, but the more immediate reason is that he wants to take a first peek at the property – right from his office computer. While talking to the new client, he plugs the address into Google Earth and zooooooooms in – North America, the West Coast, and Oregon.

"I can tell someone a lot in five minutes," Millison says. Looking at the greater landscape, then the major landforms, and finally the property itself, the permaculture designer quickly gains an understanding of the system in which the piece of land his client called about is embedded. "I usually start zoomed out and then zoom in . . . all the way down to the client," he explains. "I try to understand where they are, in a psychological sense, and what the best way to communicate with them is. I ask myself, how can I serve them?"

Before Millison, who works mainly with large-scale farms, meets a new client, he spends about an hour researching the property and the landscape surrounding it. "Where's the water coming from, and where is it going?" he wants to know. "What's upstream and around the property? How is the soil?" Often, he studies a flood plain map, too, in order to get a better sense of the watershed. When Millison analyzes a new site, he constantly zooms in and out to understand the larger ecosystem. He examines the drainage bases, the ridges, and the hilltops – the natural landscape divisions that shape the system.

"When I look at a property, I look at the patterns and the landscape. They don't exist in a grid," Millison explains. These artificial lines and demarcation are what humans have invented. This is why he believes it is necessary to take his horticulture students on field trips where they can experience the landscape in all three dimensions instead of in a two-dimensional space as it is commonly done in the classroom with maps and textbooks. "You can't teach systems in a flat space!" Millison even brings his students to his house to show them: "This is who I am." He feels it is vital to "bring his lessons to life" or, using a quote from his wife who teaches at a Waldorf School, to "live into the material." Whether he teaches or designs, Millison's objective is to "engage the whole human."

"A permaculture garden" he concludes, "teaches many lessons. It is a place to connect with soil and feel the security of producing one's food in a way that is beneficial to nature. I learn so much from being in my garden, and watching it change season to season, year to year. It is the place where I am a direct part of the web of life, and it brings me a lot of good feelings to tend my garden. And I produce a lot of food there as well, and help feed my family and community from my small plot. It brings me peace on a lot of levels: physical, mental and spiritual. The productive capacity of an intensive permaculture garden is quite astounding as well!"

THE ACHIEVEMENT

You think from systems. You flexibly zoom in and out on issues, i.e. you think analytically and holistically in turn or even simultaneously.

This means:

- *You zoom in: you analyze your work in all details, taking into account all separate parts and aspects of the system your work is related to.*
- *And you zoom out: you regard all those details together as one system. Besides, you are able to position this system within its surroundings, i.e. you treat it as a part of an even larger system.*
- *This zooming in and out is done by you regularly and fluently. As a result, you pay continuous attention to both minor details and the larger whole.*

A system literally is a whole that is composed of constituting elements that interact with each other. The company you may be working for is such a system and also the department within it, as systems often consist of smaller systems while simultaneously being a part of larger systems. A house, a refrigerator, and a human being are systems, too, just like an association, a city, a country, or a continent, a road network, the telephone network, and the Internet.

An ecosystem – as the word says – is also a system: a backyard, a forest, Yellowstone National Park, or the Everglades, as well as the ecological structure throughout California or even North America. And of course, there are virtual systems, for example, a working group cooperating through the Internet or a group of a hundred thousand gamers all over the world playing a MMORPG, a *massively multiplayer online role playing game*.

The environment of a system may be the immediate physical or societal surroundings, but it may also be a virtual environment, such as the business or intellectual network in which cooperation or competition takes place. For a house, the environment is the street, the city, the country, or the world. For a refrigerator: the kitchen in which it stands, or the house, the street, et cetera. And for the human being: the household, the larger family, the circle of friends or the sphere of professional activities, the community, the country, planet Earth – or even – the entire universe.

Professionals – ranging from, for example, mechanical engineers to prime ministers or presidents – have a tendency to zoom in during a task to the part of the system in which the work takes place. At some moments, this is fine, but preferably the attention does not stay there. When you build a house, you will hopefully have an overall design in mind. At some moment in time, you may be attaching a floorboard, and no doubt you will focus your attention on the nails or screws that you use. However, when the floor is ready, you will stand straight and look at the full result – not just the floor – but the entire house. This is zooming out, when you consider the complete system from a helicopter view. One moment you act analytically, zooming in on the details. The other moment you act holistically, focusing on the larger whole. A good professional possesses the mental flexibility to shift between both on a regular basis.

When you compare a variety of systems, you will find parallels between several of them. Navigating the healthcare system can feel like entering the burrows of a mole maze. An economic system has resemblances with an ecological system, and a roads system with the Internet and with an anthill. So you will discover regularities and rules applicable to several of them. Such comparisons help to design and construct the human world in a sustainable way, for example, by arranging cities and industrial areas using principles that are copied from nature (biomimicry). Closing material cycles is an appealing example of this.

6.2 SOURCES OF VIGOR AGAINST WEAVING FAULTS

A human being is a source of vigor for sustainability. Take Ricci Silberman, a physician assistant from Arizona, who believes that practicing medicine is "potentially very sustainable." Having worked with patients that come from "an underserved population that either has no health insurance due to financial constraints or problems getting proper immigration status," the physician assistant speaks with the experience that comes from treating inner-city patients for nearly 30 years.

Silberman, who co-owns a family practice in downtown Tucson, recognizes flaws in the system: "A significant number of my patients are undereducated and seem to have minimal understanding of personal health and prevention of disease. The most common diagnoses that I see patients for are diabetes, hypertension, hyperlipidemia, and morbid obesity. Their lifestyles are sedentary, and they exercise minimally. Their choice of foods is usually high-fat, with loads of bad carbohydrates and increased sugar. Hence, this is the reason for all of the diagnoses that they present with."

Many of Silberman's patients are clearly at risk, and it often seems that the odds are stacked against them. "Heart disease is the number one killer in the United States," she explains. Why then does she still feel that medical practitioners like her can find the sources of vigor against systemic weaving faults? The reason is that she "strongly believes in teaching personal responsibility." If these four diagnoses were treated appropriately, Silberman argues, the numbers of deaths from heart disease would decrease.

That, however, turns out to be challenging. "It is easy for me to prescribe medications, but it doesn't change the personal choices that people make. This can be very frustrating as a medical provider because I repeat the same information day in and day out." Even though it does not happen as often as she would like it to, Silberman's persistence has an impact. Occasionally, she will have patients who have turned around their lifestyle and started exercising and losing weight and making better choices with foods. "What happened?" Silberman will ask during a follow-up visit. "You really started taking care of yourself." To which her patient responds, "You told me I needed to." At this point, Silberman often thinks to herself, "I have told the last 500 patients the same thing, and they haven't listened." Yet, she reached this person, so Silberman knows she is on the right path.

It takes a lot of patience and conviction to stay on that path. "Over the years, I have attended many conferences," Silberman contends. "Usually, there is a class on learning to educate our patients in a safe, nonthreatening and nonjudgmental way. I have tried many different techniques to impart this information. Of course, the non-judgmental is heard more clearly, but I am not sure that the end result is any different."

The best results are obtained when patients recognize that the solution to the problem lies within them. This realization shapes Silberman's view on the potential for sustainability in medicine: "Patients that take personal responsibility don't need to rely on the medical system as much for medication and many follow-up appointments. If we had a healthier population, our overall healthcare would not cost as much, and we could focus on prevention of disease as opposed to spending all of our time on treatment of disease."

Aside from convincing patients to become actively involved in their own health, Silberman thinks medical providers can address the flaws in the insurance system: "In this country, there are many better avenues for sustainability and healthcare than what we currently utilize. One of the problems is what our health insurance covers. I think there is a venue for alternative medicine to be involved. I wish that our basic healthcare coverage integrated holistic medicine with allopathic medicine to help people even further."

Silberman has evidence that such approaches work. She has discovered a source of vigor, volunteering for *Grounds for Health*, an organization that practices sustainable medicine in communities that grow coffee. The physician assistant has traveled to Tanzania and Ethiopia to screen women for cervical cancer, the number one killer in women in Third World countries. "This is because they have no access to Pap smears," she points out. "A method called the single vision method was developed to use in low-resource settings. It entails using household vinegar on a patient's cervix and waiting a minute or two. If the patient has an HPV lesion – the most common reason women develop cervical cancer – we will treat that patient by freezing the lesion."

Grounds for Health donates the supplies and the units to freeze the lesions. They also offer transportation and help with treatment if a patient presents with a cancer. "By working with the local people in these countries and training the local providers, we have been able to help local practitioners take over and evaluate and treat many women in rural areas in the country where they usually wouldn't have access to this screening," Silberman says. "The national health departments in Tanzania and Ethiopia support the practitioners with resources. So then our work is done, and the program becomes sustainable."

THE ACHIEVEMENT

You recognize flaws in the fabric and sources of vigor in systems, and you use the sources of vigor.

This means:

- *You are aware, or you investigate, which flaws in the fabric are deeply integrated in the systems with which or for which you work. These flaws are the ultimate causes of un-sustainability.*

- *You discover which sources of vigor are available in or around these systems in order to correct the flaws in the fabric. These sources of vigor are the powers we possess toward true sustainability.*
- *You succeed in effectively utilizing or mobilizing the sources of vigor, enabling you to diminish or even eradicate the flaws, or at least to decrease the negative consequences of them.*

Recognizing flaws in the fabric and sources of vigor is similar to making a SWOT analysis. The letters SWOT stand for Strengths, Weaknesses, Opportunities, and Threats. The concept is well known in business. When it comes to sustainability, you perform such an analysis more fundamentally than what would be usual and with more than average attention to the long-term future. Often the Triple-P is applied: "people," "planet," and "profit."

Of course, it is preferable to use the conclusions of such an analysis to start real improvements. This requires inspiration, leadership, and vision. It is amazing how many acres of monoculture are beginning to be transformed into permaculture. And think of how many women have escaped cancer because of early intervention methods. Professionals like Andrew Millison and Ricci Silberman can inspire many students, patients, and colleagues every year. If only a part of them will be able to integrate elements of sustainability within their academic study and in their profession, the impact will be enormous. That is how to get a lot of sustainably competent professionals!

6.3 IN THE CHAIN, IN THE LOOP

In 2006, Will Robben bought a cable equipment company that sold equipment for laying cables of all sorts. Within three years, Will thoroughly revamped the company, increasing the turnover by 60%. He did this in such an innovative way that he received two prestigious industry awards.

The company was thriving until the economic crisis broke out in 2009, which brought severe consequences for Robben's business. The building and construction sector collapsed, and big customers quickly left – one after another. At the beginning of 2011, Robben's company was legally declared bankrupt. This was the moment when Will started rethinking everything he had done before.

In brief, his conclusion came down to the following: his former customers had a need for certain equipment that they used to buy from his company. The machines Robben had acquired were in use for several hours, but actually most of the time, they were standing still, doing nothing. Wasn't this a waste, from a sustainability viewpoint? If arranged properly, two or three companies might be able to share just one machine, which would save a lot of things: resources, energy, and construction costs for the production of quite a few machines (that would sit idle most of the time.)

But, hey! Which production company would start to actively promote selling *fewer* products? Suddenly, a switch flipped in Will Robben's head.

Why had companies bought machines from his cable equipment company before it went bankrupt? Because they wanted to *own* the equipment? Certainly not. Because they wanted to *use* it? If that was the case, buying the devices was not at all necessary. You could rent them, couldn't you? Fine, but if everyone prefers to rent the devices and no one owns them, there isn't much to be rented, right? So, what if you start with the companies that already possess the equipment? If you could set up a network consisting of those companies and the companies that might want to lease the machinery, you could perhaps become the mediator who connects the two companies and enables the lease – only for limited amounts of time, aiming at common use of the equipment. This would be good for the people renting since they would not have to buy expensive machines but could instead rent them for much less money. It would also be good for the lenders, who bought the machines for a lot of money, as they would be able to get a return on their investment.

No sooner said than done. In 2011, Will started his new company, Floow2, which does exactly what I described. For example, it mediates between large farms, making it possible for agricultural equipment standing idle on a certain farm to be temporarily leased to other farmers. The same is happening with machines for forestry, cranes, and equipment for road construction.

Robben found an opportunity to look beyond an apparent need of companies (buying equipment) to a much more fundamental need (being able to use equipment now and then). All he had to do was transition from selling *products* to delivering *services*. That freed him from the economic necessity to sell as much as possible, and it gave him the opportunity to contribute to fewer products in a way that was feasible from a business economics viewpoint. Floow2 is doing great, and thanks to this success, Robben contributes in two ways: to ecological and economic sustainability.

THE ACHIEVEMENT

You think and act in an integrated, chain-oriented, or even circular way.

This means:

- *You deliver services, products, or processes. You describe how they are a part of a larger whole, e.g. of a chain or a life cycle in which many others, perhaps in different companies or countries, are working – before or after you – in the chain.*
- *Your activities may concern the life cycle of an industrial product, a human being, an animal, a natural habitat, a company, a community, or a country, etc. You may, for example, think of your suppliers and your customers.*
- *You map the consequences for sustainable development of these services, products, or processes, and you relate them to the total of the consequences of the entire chain or life cycle.*
- *You cooperate on improvement of these consequences with others who control or influence other parts of the chain.*
- *You design entirely new ways to fulfill the same functions and needs, and you conclude whether they are better than the existing ones considering sustainable development.*

The transition from products to services can be seen in many fields at the moment. Take for instance "pay per lux," a principle that was developed by Philips in collaboration with architect Thomas Rau. According to this principle, as a company, you don't buy lamps but rather light. (Hence the name: "lux" is a measure for luminance or brightness.) That is to say, Philips designs the illumination scheme in the laboratories and offices of a customer based on the customer's needs. Philips installs the armatures and lamps. Philips also pays for the electricity, replaces failing lamps, and adapts the lighting when the company changes. In other words, Philips is no longer a product seller but a service provider. There are many advantages. The customer, a company paying "per lux," doesn't have to take care of the lighting anymore since the service provider guarantees that everything works. In the past, some people used to say that light bulbs were produced in such a way that they would fail sooner rather than later (planned obsolescence); otherwise, the light bulb industry would not make enough money. Well, with the new approach, planned obsolescence is unthinkable because if the lights don't last, the only one suffering is the provider itself. The provider also has an advantage: instead of a one-time contract while selling lamps, the provider now establishes an ongoing connection with customers, who will stay as long as they are satisfied.

We're talking about a true transition here. If many goods are delivered in this way, not through sales but as rent or lease, with a maintenance obligation attached, the entire economy will change, even for ordinary household and lawn service clients. Try to remember the last time your washing machine broke down. Did you have a repairperson or a new machine in the house on the same or even the following day? If you did, maybe you were lucky. Probably you didn't. However, if instead of buying a washing machine you had acquired a laundry contract, it would be in the immediate interest of the provider to replace the machine soon – and with a darn good model that is – since the provider has to pay a penalty for every day on which you cannot do laundry. When this principle is also applied to cars (as it has become quite customary), bicycles, kitchen equipment, TV's, computers, printers, haymakers, threshers, printing presses, and folding machines, the economic and societal impacts are huge.

The nice thing is that I am not making this up. Many experts expect that this is all going to happen, or rather, it is already going on at full speed. We call it "the circular economy." If you are not yet familiar with the concept, google it. You will be amazed.

The consequences for sustainability are great because the producers of the goods remain their owners. You don't have to discuss deposits or take-back obligations because the taking back part is woven into the system. This "design for disassembly" method automatically convinces companies to design products in a manner that at their end-of-life point, when the devices are worn or obsolete, they can easily be taken apart. This makes it possible to reuse certain components or to recycle the material (see *the product designer* in Chapter 11). Closing the loop has become inevitable, and you automatically arrive at C2C, cradle to cradle!

Besides this "technological cycle," there is the "biological cycle," in which the resources with which the technological cycle starts are derived from nature and in which, at the end of the life of a product, its waste materials are returned to nature in such a way that nature is not harmed. Together, the two cycles form a kind of figure "8." You can see this "8" in Figure 6.2, lying on its side. The figure is derived from the second edition of my university textbook *Fundamentals of Sustainable Development*, (Routledge, 2017). In that book, you can find many more theoretical details about the circular economy.

In principle, this circularity idea is all highly logical and easy. In reality, it becomes more complicated when the chain of involved companies and customers is long and complex. When you are dealing with resources that are harvested or mined somewhere in the world, shipped to a broker, then combined into components consisting of several materials that are put together to form complex devices, etc., it can be very difficult to close the cycles. It will only be possible if the various links in the chain cooperate closely according to the principles of "integral chain management." Fortunately, there exist thousands of examples to document the success of this method. As a percentage of the worldwide economy, the circular economy is growing at an explosive rate, and within a decade it will have gained critical mass.

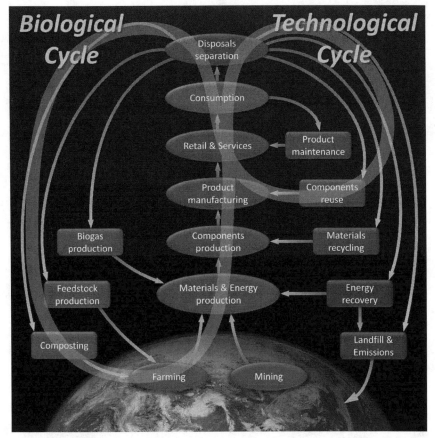

Figure 6.2 *The two cycles of a Circular Economy*

Wonderful, beautiful! But what about the traditional service providers, for example, in healthcare? Well, in those fields, it is also possible to talk about an integral approach if caregivers cooperate with each other to provide suitable services, not to a knee or kidney, but to a human being. Moreover, if teachers and instructors of primary, secondary, and higher education start coordinating their work with institutions for lifelong learning, an integrated, chain-oriented, or even circular approach is born – aimed not at the lifecycle of products but of people. Cradle to cradle is not a proper term here, unless you consider the beds in the homes for the elderly a kind of cradle. In a figurative sense, the term does fit: people who reach old age have gone from intensive care (as a baby) to independency (as an adult) back again to intensive care (as an elderly person). Cycle closed.

CHAPTER SEVEN

Levels of competence

Think about it. You are either competent, or you're not? Of course, in reality, it's neither; rather, you can be more – or less – competent. A person may be a well-educated and experienced professional who is held in high esteem by everyone, or a novice who has learned quite a few things but doesn't have much practical experience yet. A suitable model is the medieval concept of the master and the apprentice. The former has mastered the profession deeply. The latter is only allowed to work, for the time being, under the supervision of the master. He or she still has to acquire more skills and is not yet considered competent in the discipline.

To describe the sustainability competences, I will use more than just the two competence levels that the medieval guilds applied. I distinguish seven levels. You can utilize them to assess your own personal competences. In the closing chapters of this book, I will offer you a concrete instrument for this purpose.

LEVEL 1: APPRENTICE

At the first level, you are an apprentice or a student. You have not yet gathered sufficient competences to practice your profession. You may assist your more experienced colleagues or teachers in the execution of their jobs, the main goal of which is not that you realize concrete achievements, but that you learn from your tasks. You may perform some of your activities in simulated work circumstances instead of real ones. Whenever you do work in a real professional context, your primary obligation is not to produce a result but to show your effort.

LEVEL 2: WORK UNDER SUPERVISION

At the second level, you are able to perform your job fully or partially – under supervision. You are the "journeyman," the trainee who is able to achieve solid results with the aid of experienced colleagues.

A typical example in the healthcare field would be the recent medical school graduate who is completing a residency under the supervision of a medical specialist.

LEVEL 3: SELF-DIRECT

At the third level, you are able to bring into practice what you have learned as a self-directed professional. Not more, not less. At a practical level, you perform tasks that are in line with the usual demands of your profession. Your vision, your opinions, and your activities are mainly related to your personal expertise, your immediate work environment, and the customary work methods. Creativity is not demanded and generally not even appreciated.

LEVEL 4: INTEGRATE

At the fourth level, you are able to position your work within a wider context and benefit from that. In the performance of your job, you navigate a complex range of topics, work styles, persons, and cultures. You may do this:

- *beyond the limits of your own expertise;*
- *taking into consideration different cultures, value systems, traditions;*
- *beyond the usual expectations and work methods of your profession; and/or*
- *in flexibly changing roles, e.g. managing.*

LEVEL 5: IMPROVE

At the fifth level, you are able to implement concrete improvements in the work that you and others are doing. You oversee – both at a detailed level and at a systems level – your work and the system within which you perform your professional activities. You judge your own work and that of others with whom you cooperate critically, and you estimate its consequences in the widest sense. Based on that, you constantly aim at improving the work to which you contribute, and in doing so, you achieve noticeable results.

LEVEL 6: INNOVATE

At the sixth level, you are the source of innovation within your discipline. You introduce innovative insights into your work, concerning:

- *the goals or targets that have been set;*
- *the means and methods that are applied;*
- *the effects of the work;*
- *the scope of those effects in space and time;*
- *the underlying vision; and*
- *the relations inside and outside of your work environment or your discipline, e.g.: society as a whole.*

These innovations are demonstrably visible in your professional activities and in their results.

LEVEL 7: MASTER

At the highest level, you are prominent within your discipline. You have reached "mastership." Others learn from you. You are their role model, their "archetype." Your inspiring leadership is recognized and accepted by all. Such masters are extremely rare. You may think of Nobel Prize winners and Oscar winners, or others who perhaps have not won official awards, but who are recognized at a conference or meeting because when they start talking, everybody else becomes silent and listens. Probably, you can name one of a few of those special persons within your own professional sector.

In order to contribute to sustainable development, you don't have to be a master. The stories in this book prove that *every* professional, working at *whatever* level, can be a sustainability hero.

CHAPTER EIGHT
Future orientation

The Competence (Figure 8.1):

A sustainably competent professional thinks and acts on the basis of a perspective of the future.

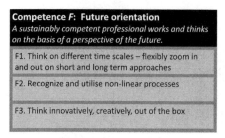
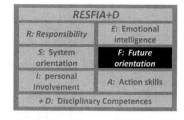

Figure 8.1 *Competence F: Future orientation*

You probably spend a lot of time in cars, perhaps at the steering wheel. You make sure that your front window is clean and clear so that you can constantly see where you are heading. If this is not the case – perhaps you covered the windshield because of severe frost to prevent ice crystals – and you start driving while the cover is still on, you won't get very far. A hundred yards later, you will probably end up wrapped around a lamppost, or worse, you'll hit another car or a child crossing the street. Of course, nobody would do that. You would be a fool if you did, you don't go on the road *blindly*!

Have you ever realized that when riding in a car, you actually travel in two directions at once? First, when you drive on the road, you cover a *distance* expressed in miles or kilometers. Second, while you drive, you also move in *time*, and this is expressed in minutes or hours. Even if you are standing still, not adding any miles to your traveling distance, your temporal motion continues: hour upon hour, day by day, year after year. Why, then, do so many people travel *blindly* toward the future?

It's funny. Sometimes when I present to an audience, I ask a couple of people where they want to be in ten years, or in 25? What do they wish to have accomplished? Which dreams would they want to have fulfilled?

Who would they want to be by then? Almost every time, these people seem to be surprised: they never thought about it. Usually, they like the question all right, and they start thinking out loud. Please do the same and ask somebody you meet this question. You will see what a remarkable conversation you will have. By the way, what would *you* say if I posed the question to you?

A comparable question can be asked at a different level. I tend to ask entrepreneurs – if possible, in front of a large audience since it always leads to fascinating dialogues – why they think their companies will still exist in twenty years. Without exception, the reactions are interesting, and nearly every time, you will see that the interviewee has never even thought about it. So, you get something like this: "Of course, my company will still exist 'cause I deliver excellent products or services!"

Right. It's always beautiful to see how an entrepreneur believes in his or her own product, but whether that is sufficient is doubtful. What if, between now and in twenty years, this excellent product becomes obsolete or is outperformed by something even better or cheaper? What if the people twenty years from now just don't need your product, excellent as it may be? Yes, entrepreneurs who don't think about such things travel *blindly* toward the future.

Is society as a whole also blind to the future? Sometimes it is, sometimes it isn't. Of course, you can't predict the future. But at least you can think about it, and that happens surprisingly seldom. Future blindness is what you see all around. Like when national politicians discuss political decisions with extremely long consequence periods without the people in the country participating in a general discussion concerning their wishes about what the country should look like in 50 years. For example, how much wealthier would they want to be by that time? Future blindness is also seen when oil companies happily report that oil fields under the oceanic bed of the North Pole will soon be exploitable as – thanks to global warming – the polar ice will disappear entirely during the summer.

"You would be a fool," I just wrote. "You don't go on the road *blindly*!" Well we do, and more than just sometimes.

This chapter is about the dimension of "time." It's the complement of the former chapter, in which "place" had the key role. Below are the three achievements I will describe:

- *Think in different time scales – flexibly zoom in and out of short- and long-term approaches*
- *Recognize and utilize non-linear processes*
- *Think innovatively, creatively, and out of the box*

8.1 SHORT- AND LONG-TERM

It was an emerging crisis. As Miami Beach was bracing itself for yet another October king tide, when streets routinely flood even though no cloud is in sight, Mayor Philip Levine announced on the city's public TV channel, "We have storms. We have rising sea level, due to climate change, but we're taking the offensive, aggressive action to making sure our city is viable and livable for the next 500 years at a minimum."

The person at the center of helping Miami Beach realize these ambitious plans is the city's new Chief Resiliency Officer, Susy Torriente. "I'm not an engineer and not a scientist," Torriente says. "I'm a communicator and collaborator. I am giving our experts the tools we need." Working both on an operational and a strategic level means she has to recognize interconnections, she says.

Ideally, short- and long-term perspectives should be intertwined in a natural way. So how does one tackle long-term sustainability issues such as sea level rise? Torriente shares her approach: "These issues may be 50–100 years out, but in local government, you deal with a one-year budget and election cycles. The first plan I worked on was a five-year plan, but I would always bring it back to looking at short-term solutions and ask, how do you break it down into segments? It's a matter of what's doable." Working in a political environment often means seizing opportunities when they arise, as different administrations can be more or less supportive. "When the stars align," Torriente says, "it is time to push forward."

Torriente thinks that aside from being aware of how government works, a vital skill for city managers like her is to have the ability to zoom in and out to see the big picture. "You have to observe, listen to the experts, and make connections . . . I ask incoming young city interns to close their eyes and imagine the city in 30 years when they are going to be in the top position." Innovation plays a significant role, too. The need drives innovation," Torriente believes. "We have to challenge ourselves, and we have to take risks. We're writing the 'textbook' now. We need to train our staff and build capacity. In the face of climate change, we have to deliver services differently." NOAA (National Oceanic and Atmospheric Association), for example, offers climate awareness training, she notes. Torriente also embraces creative solutions. In addition to traditional "gray infrastructure," she increasingly promotes "green infrastructure, such as dunes and living shorelines" to create a natural environment that can protect residents.

Before accepting the position in Miami Beach, Torriente served as Assistant City Manager in Ft. Lauderdale and participated in a program called CityLinks, a collaboration between South Florida and Durban, South Africa, another coastal city threatened by rising sea levels. Torriente, who has also attended resiliency meetings in Canada and Germany, accomplished several goals. She was able to converse with international experts to disseminate best practices and also to share her insights when she was invited to teach a course to Durban's municipal employees, a unique experience she found "very exciting and rewarding since they can now replicate our strategies and action from South Florida to South Africa." Durban is implementing a climate compact based on South Florida's model.

What Miami Beach or the many other affected coastal areas will look like in 500 years cannot be foretold, but with someone like Susy Torriente in charge, the city's residents and the mayor alike can face the next king tide knowing that 1-year, 5-year, 20-year, and 100-year adaptation and mitigation plans to counteract the impact are in place.

THE ACHIEVEMENT

You think on different time scales, distinguishing between a short-term and a long-term approach.

This means:

- *You zoom in: you analyze the opportunities and consequences of your work for the short term.*
- *Your short-term approach to the problem is aimed at tackling symptoms. (This is the operational approach).*
- *You also zoom out: you investigate the options for the long term, if necessary even years ahead, to improve your work fundamentally and in an innovative way.*
- *Where solving problems is the issue, you primarily aim at eradicating their causes. (This is the strategic approach).*
- *This zooming in and out in time is done by you regularly and fluently, thanks to which you have continuous attention for both the short- and the long-term.*

Zooming in and out in time is easy to understand if you imagine the following situation. You are sitting quietly at home one night. Outside it is raining cats and dogs, but inside it feels nice and cozy until you suddenly realize that water is dripping from the ceiling. The roof is leaking! What do you do? Well, or course, the very first thing you do is get towels, wipe up the water, and place some buckets. The leaking roof is one thing, but you don't want your costly hardwood floor or broadloom carpet to get ruined as well.

Next, you have to find the cause. Something is wrong with the roof. Maybe some roof tiles have shifted, or perhaps a watertight strip is no longer watertight. In other words, you find the cause and repair the damage. You might even take another big step and replace the entire roof, or as a last resort, you may find another house and move. Wiping water up with towels and placing buckets – these are examples of short-term actions. They don't address the causes, but they prevent further damage. This is what acting *operationally* means.

Repairing the roof represents a more profound approach. If you don't do it, you will still be emptying buckets next year. It is a *tactical* approach, aimed at a longer term than the towel operation. It's not a matter of minutes; rather, it takes days or weeks.

When you replace the roof or even move to another place altogether, then you apply a genuine long-term view. We call this a *strategic* approach, which involves considering many issues, not just acute problems. For example, you would ask yourself, "How do I want to live in twenty years?"

To put it a bit more formally:

A *strategic* policy aims at the long term, endeavoring to realize fundamental goals based on the mission of an organization or on personal life goals.

A *tactical* policy aims at an intermediate term, attempting to realize concrete targets of the organization or of a person, possibly (but not necessarily) derived from the strategic policy.

An *operational* policy makes use of methods that can be applied immediately or in the short term, possibly (but not necessarily) based on tactical or strategic plans.

How long is long term? It's impossible to define it in an absolute sense; it depends on the context. For businesses or communities, the guidelines are as follows:

Short = now or in less than six months to two years
Intermediate = three to five years
Long = up to 20 or 100 years (or more)

> Many exceptions to these rules exist. For example, if the roof is
> leaking, repairs (= intermediate to long-term) occur within a
> matter of days or weeks at the most – I hope.

A sustainably competent professional is able to oversee and connect
these various terms, from short to long, in a harmonious way.

An earlier competence from Chapter 6 dealt with "Parts and wholes." In
that section, I described how you zoom in and out within a system, from
its details to a helicopter view and back. The same approach, alternating
between the analytical and the holistic view, is not only needed within
the dimension of *space*, but also with the other dimension: *time*.

Focusing on the immediate future (the king tide causing flooding
next week) while also envisioning the future of the next generation
(12 inches of predicted sea level rise over the coming decades means
causeways and bridges need to be elevated) and being able to flexibly
move from one time frame to the other – that is what a sustainable
professional does.

This is not easy because the short term usually draws more attention
than the long term. Many politicians look only to the next election,
managers to the upcoming shareholder meeting, and employees to
their approaching performance review. From sustainable professionals
you may expect better. Do you remember the "rule of thumb for
making sound decisions" in Chapter 2? It deals with the distinction
between short- and long-term. The long-term consequences should
always weigh in. What is your opinion about, let's say, the extraction of
shale gas, for which the ground has to be fracked – that is "shattered?"
What will people think about fracking in 100 years? Maybe they will
think it's all right that we did this for a few decades, maybe not. What
is your guess?

Someone who does not want to travel blindly toward the future,
someone who does not want to crash or accidentally hit a child in ten
or 100 years, looks ahead and anticipates in order to reach an agreeable
future. *This is the very first principle of sustainable development.*

8.2 NOT JUST LINEAR

1 + 1 = 2, right? That's what you learn in school, and 10 + 10 = 20, 20 + 20 = 40, and so on. It's not just theory; you can see it in real life all around you, too. That is, if you don't see past the end of your nose. Please take a look:

1   *Soccer: When I sign players that cost twice as much, my team will score twice as many goals. 1 + 1 = 2.*

2   *Merger: When I double the size of my company through a merger, the overhead will double, too (and therefore stay the same, relatively speaking). 1 + 1 = 2.*

3   *Money: When I am twice as rich, I will be twice as happy. 1 + 1 = 2.*

4   *Traffic: When I double the number of lanes on a highway, twice as many cars can pass without causing a traffic jam. 1 + 1 = 2.*

5   *Criminality: When I double the punishment, safety will increase by 100% as well: 1 + 1 = 2, so crime rates will halve.*

Dear reader, no doubt it is clear to you that these kinds of "laws" are incorrect. I call them *doubling laws*. They are hardly ever true, and so perhaps they should rather be called *doubling myths*. Intuitively, we all think, now and then, that processes will develop "normally" and won't result in anything unexpected. Our instincts are tuned this way. As a rule, we expect linear relations. In other words, when something is doubled, some other thing will double, too.

Such linear thinking can also be found in a more figurative sense, not literally as a doubling law or a myth. Reality is supposed to be simple and easy even though it is actually more complicated. I will give you a few examples:

6   *Healthcare: When the citizens of a country become healthier, medical expenses will decrease.*

7   *Competition: When commercial competition is introduced in service sectors such as public transportation or healthcare, the quality of these services will improve.*

8 **Nature**: *People have evolved from nature, so when I buy and eat natural products, I will be healthier.*

9 **Conservation of misery**: *War, poverty, and hunger will never be eradicated from the Earth because they have always been there. There is nothing new under the sun. History just repeats itself.*

10 **Medical technology**: *In a few decades, we will be able to extend human life expectancy to 150 years.*

One of the characteristics of sustainably competent professionals is that they don't naively believe in such simplifications of reality. They don't fall for easy thinking errors; they dig deeper. Reality is almost always non-linear.

When I was thinking about a good way to illustrate this principle with a story from real life, I soon arrived at the example of *traffic*. Traffic conceals a lot of non-linear traps, concerning themes such as velocity, energy consumption, safety, congestion, and more.

The "braking distance," the number of feet you need to stop your car completely, presents a clear example. When you watch the behavior of drivers on the highway, you get the impression that many of them, especially the tailgaters, think the braking distance is (at the most) linearly proportional to the velocity – in other words, a doubling law. However, it isn't. At a speed of about 40 mph, a realistic breaking distance is 76 feet (in dry weather conditions). At a twice as high velocity, 80 mph, the breaking distance increases to more than 300 feet: four times as large. That's not all. If a line of cars is moving on the highway and just one driver plays with his cellphone, causing him to take two extra seconds to react, his breaking distance shoots up to around 550 feet! Bad luck for those behind him. If something happens that requires the entire line of cars to stop quickly, not just this single driver will suffer, but – thanks to him – many others who did drive carefully.

Thinking about traffic, I came to the conclusion that there is only one person I know who is able to explain these things the best: "Mister Traffic" himself. A Dutch TV personality well known for his peppy remarks, Koos Spee, a.k.a. Mister Traffic, served as a district attorney until his retirement and was responsible for the Netherland's national traffic policy for many years, advising government ministers and directors. Once, Mister Traffic commented on a young motorcyclist who did not seem to know the traffic regulations: "In my opinion, it's been quite a few years that people could win their driver's license in a game of dominoes. Nowadays, you actually need to pass a test for it, so I think, he was pretending to be more ignorant than he actually is." On another occasion, Spee made remarks about young men who spend a lot of money to embellish their cars (in their own eyes). "Yes, I perfectly understand," he said in a wry tone. "Those boys put their heart and soul into it, and it may cost some. There will come a time when they need all that money for something else, and then it will end all by itself."

I sent Spee an email with a request for an interview for my book, and I received a kind reply from him, inviting me to come to his home. And so, on a nice morning, I was sitting on the porch in the backyard of Koos Spee's house. I had prepared myself by reading one of his books in which he writes ironically: "I can imagine that as a cyclist you don't always see the necessity to stop at a red traffic light, but many of those who passed the stop signal are now parking on the wrong side of the grass" (or six feet under).

In his online blog, Spee cracks a few doubling myths. One of them goes like this: if all motorists would drive twice as fast, twice as many cars could pass the road. Is this true? Of course, it isn't. In reality, you will get maximum road capacity of a highway when everybody drives at 50 mph. When we try to travel with 75 mph, we get jolts and jerks, accelerating and braking – congestion. In symbolic math: $50 + 25 = 30$.

During the interview, I started talking about widening a highway by adding extra lanes, a practice that is also very popular in the United States, where space is so abundant. When my co-author Anouchka Rachelson, who lives in the United States, read this, she immediately agreed and remarked, "Right now, they are widening the four lanes of a highway near my house to six lanes, which won't ease the congestion but just invite more people to ride on the highway." This is myth number 4 in my list above. Spee said, "Yeah, look. If everybody behaved rationally, a twice as wide highway might indeed double the capacity, but that is not what happens as most people have a tendency to drive in the left lane. That leaves a large part of the road capacity unused."

Halfway through the interview, I mentioned myth number 5 (in the list above), regarding raising punishments and penalties. Many people have the expectation that this would lead to better behavior in traffic, but not Koos Spee. "Raise penalties? That doesn't work at all!" he says emphatically. "The probability of detection, that's the only thing that really works." He adds a splendid metaphor. "In the Middle Ages punishments were extremely heavy. Pickpockets were hung publicly at the center of the town square. But let me tell you, never were more pockets picked than during such an execution! So, the probability of detection matters, not the size of the penalty. The *subjective* probability that is. Pain in the purse! If people believe they won't get caught, they don't change their behavior. Speed traps with recognizable police cars or with speed cameras in fixed positions hardly help because then people know it is 'safe' further down the road, so I gave unmarked cars of different brands and models to all police departments. They swap them now and then to prevent motorists from recognizing them in the long run."

After the interview, I drove home observing traffic carefully. So many lanes! And yes indeed, the right lane only carried the odd truck and the rest of it was empty. Even the second lane was hardly used. Most motorists were engaged in a kind of battle for the two lanes on the left. Me too!

In 1996, Spee started as the national district attorney for traffic, and two years later he founded the Bureau for Traffic Enforcement. This had an immediate effect on the Netherland's traffic policy. During Spee's tenure, the number of traffic fatalities was cut in half. Of course, this reduction was not due to Spee alone. Here too, it is not as simple as $1 + 1 = 2$. Cars have become safer over the years; however, in

neighboring countries, the number of fatalities decreased far less –
until a few years ago when these countries adopted Spee's traffic
policy. You can safely say that Koos Spee saved hundreds of lives,
although you will never be able to point at those whose lives have been
spared because they did *not* have an accident.

In recent years, environmental quality related to traffic has gotten a
lot of political attention. Spee tells the story of a conversation with
a cabinet member: "She wanted to set the speed limit on one of the
highways at 45 mph because a nearby village had a lot of trouble with
exhaust gases. It appeared that residents inhaled the equivalent of 17
cigarettes each day. I said to the representative: You shouldn't do that
because then big trucks will constantly shift gears, down and up, down
and up. From all this breaking and accelerating, exhaust will actually
increase. You won't have that with a limit of 50 mph instead 45 mph.
So if you want me to uphold the law, I am fully prepared to do so, but
only if you make it 50 – and that is what happened." Spee's anecdote
serves as a nice example of a non-linear effect: Sometimes, considering
the emission, 45 is larger than 50.

Concluding the fascinating interview – Spee could have gone on for
hours telling me many more interesting stories – I asked him, "But Koos,
this traffic enforcement, isn't that like mopping the floor while keeping
the water running? Just now when I drove from my house to yours in an
hour or so, I saw quite a few tailgaters, people on their cellphones, and
road hogs!"

"Yes," Spee replied, "but if we don't mop, we'll certainly drown."

THE ACHIEVEMENT

You recognize and utilize non-linear processes.

This means:

- *You know the difference between linear and non-linear processes:
  both in a literal and a figurative sense.*

- *You describe non-linear, perhaps unexpected developments within your own work.*
- *You make use of this distinction to realistically estimate the chances, risks, and consequences of your work.*
- *Based on that estimate, you design your work in such a way that it fits optimally with sustainability. To this purpose, you focus, for example, on the goals, the working environment, and the methods you apply.*

Rarely are causes and effects correlated linearly. That is because the systems we deal with – the road network, healthcare, the economy, the climate, etc. – are complex. Many causes, circumstances, effects, and side effects influence one another mutually. This creates feedback loops through which the effects influence the causes. Positive feedback increases the effects ($1 + 1 = 3$), negative feedback decreases them ($1 + 1 = 1 ½$, or 1, or even 0). When many such feedbacks exist, the behavior of a system can be incredibly hard to predict. That is the reason why it is impossible to reliably predict the future, where you have to deal with every imaginable system, all actively interacting with one another. You cannot simply extrapolate current trends from the past to the future; developments rarely continue as they did in the past. If, as a professional, you are sustainably competent, you know this and take it into account.

Ah, yes. Before I finish this section, you may want to know why the ten examples I mentioned are less linear than some people think. Here are the reasons.

1 **Soccer**: Adding expensive new players to a team can often be disappointing. The quality of a soccer team depends primarily on the team, rather than on individual players. If the team is strong, you may get: $1 + 1 = 5$ and the championship. If not, $1 + 1 = 1 ½$ at most. If you're unlucky: $1 + 1 = 0$ and maybe a demotion.

2 **Merger**: Alas, a bigger organization inevitably calls for more bureaucracy, formally or hidden. In this case, $1 + 1 = 3$ applies, which in this context usually is not considered a blessing.

3   **Money**: People who are really poor can be unhappy, for example, due to hunger or lack of medical care. However, beyond a certain level of prosperity, more money at best brings some extra happiness for a short while. It does not last as research has repeatedly proved. In management theory terms, money is a typical hygiene factor or work environment factor, just like washing your hands: less decreases happiness, but more does not necessarily increase it. In other words, $1 + 1 = 1$.

4   **Traffic**: You already received an important explanation from Mr. Spee. There are other reasons why extra lanes don't always lead to less congestion. For example, there could be a bottleneck on the next highway, which did not get new lanes, a bottleneck near roadwork, or a congested exit ramp. An accident that involves a truck leaking hazardous fluids and blocking the entire highway including the new lanes could be the cause. In most cases, new lanes render at best something like $1 + 1 = 1 ¼$.

5   **Criminality**: Traffic infractions are not the only area where stiffer punishment hardly ever leads to better behavior. Time after time, scientific research has proved that crime rates strongly depend on the probability of detection and far less on the severity of the punishment: $1 + 1 = 1$.

6   **Healthcare**: Many people intuitively expect that a better average state of health leads to a reduction of healthcare costs, something like $1 + 1 = 1 ½$. However, that is not correct. You see, even the people who stay healthy for more years will eventually get old and infirm, and they will cause the same medical expenses, only a few years later. In the years between, they will incur medical costs, too, albeit relatively low. The result is an increase in healthcare costs, not a decrease: $1 + 1 = 2 ½$.

7   **Competition**: When the primary goal of an organization shifts from services to profitability, it usually appears that the quality of the services decreases rather than increases.

8   **Natural**: Oh well, nicotine is a natural product, and so are cocaine and even strychnine, a popular rat poison.

9 **Conservation of misery**: Nothing new under the sun? Right. 200 years ago, people could say, "We have never flown, so that will never happen." Now look at Hartsfield-Jackson Atlanta International or Heathrow! In reality, history has never repeated itself. There is no law in nature prohibiting the eradication of war, hunger, or other misery. However, after thousands of years of bloodshed all over Europe, there has not been a war between EU countries in more than 50 years – a sensation, a unique achievement – so keep your courage and strive for peace and prosperity for all.

10 **Medical technology**: Medically seen, this may be true, but from an ecological viewpoint, it certainly is not. It would present a catastrophe! If everyone got twice as old, preserving the present health and prosperity, it would double the world population, which would go far beyond the biocapacity of our planet. Already, it will be hard enough to feed and house some eleven billion people, halfway into the twenty-first century. In reality, we would not get even close to doubling the world population because long before that, the ecological system and (hence) the economy would collapse – a global catastrophe and the deaths of billions of people: $1 + 1 = 0$. Dear medical researchers, why don't you think beyond the boundaries of your own discipline? Where is your societal responsibility?

8.3 INNOVATIVE, CREATIVE, OUT OF THE BOX

It is amazing what you can accomplish as an individual if you have the guts to take that first step, go beyond the well-known boundaries, and harness the power of community. This is most certainly true for Nick Papadopoulos, social entrepreneur and co-founder of CropMobster, an online local food network that uses crowdsourcing to prevent food waste, boost food security, and help local farmers as well as food businesses grow and gain awareness.

"One Sunday night, in 2013, I was standing in a large walk-in cooler next to a crate of premium vegetables that I knew were going to rot and be thrown out if I didn't do something about it. At that moment, I had an idea, and so I went home and started experimenting with social media to create an alert. The next morning, a mother in a minivan stopped by and picked up the food. It was a beautiful 'win-win' outcome for everyone!" Nick, who lives in the San Francisco Bay Area, remembers.

Encouraged by this experience, Papadopoulos created his crowdsourcing organization CropMobster. "I thought, all this value is being wasted. Why don't we create a model to connect people and find a home for the vegetables, turn loss into value? We built the initial website in four days. The name CropMobster was inspired by the idea of a flash mob, only one that specializes in food. The idea resonated. With a little bit of innovation and the swarm effect, it took off. When we first started, we couldn't have imagined the various ways our work would unfold for larger scale impact or challenges we would face. Now, with a few years under our belt, we have good data and a large set of experiences to define a bit more what the impacts of decisions will be."

Nick is passionate about his project: "We are becoming a local food hub and network that is helping facilitate a range of positive impacts. There are multiple benefits: we get healthy food to those in need, help local businesses drive sales, prevent food waste, keep discarded food and organic out of the landfill, and connect with an inspired community – that's when beauty happens. We're at the nexus or overlap where the sharing economy and circular economy meet."

The CropMobster website offers a variety of service categories ranging from deals, donations, trades, and more. Offerings include free compost-ready vegetables and chickens looking for a new home, gleaning gatherings during which community members can collect left-over crops such as lettuce and tomatoes, and posts to sell used tools and machinery like the recently listed John Deere 365 hay swather. In addition, there are announcements of local events such as the "Don't Chuck the Pumpkin" initiative around Halloween and trade offers like "homemade sourdough bread for persimmons."

To anticipate the needs of the community, the CropMobster team engages with its customers. Papadopoulos describes it as follows, "We try to take frequent steps back to see the forest from the trees and look at things from an interconnected systems perspective. We also spend a lot of time listening, observing in dialogue with people using our platform to understand their needs and develop creative, crowd-sourced ways to meet those needs. Finally, we try to 'stack functions' or benefits to make sure that one idea or solution has a range of positive impacts at once. When you can stack impacts and benefits, there is the opportunity to really generate momentum and make progress."

Of course, there are always moments when Nick has to make business decisions and weigh alternatives and their consequences: "When confronted with decision points or challenges, we try to list out all of the various paths or choices we could make and then list the pros and cons of each. We also try to think of various scenarios in the future. Finally, trust in our clients and community members is everything. We ask ourselves, 'Will we be building trust or degrading trust with a certain path of action?' Everything we do – whether internally as a team or with the CropMobster community – is based on trust, transparency and trying to be as authentic and real as possible."

Papadopoulos is proud of the fact that CropMobster has "inspired people and even other platforms and models to tackle the issues of food waste, food security and local farm and food business viability." For those just starting out, he recommends "Keep your costs low, and don't worry about making money at first. Instead, be a scout for problems and opportunities. Cultivate your patient listening and observation skills. Strive to identify significant 'win-win' opportunities to solve problems and create value in communities and systems."

THE ACHIEVEMENT

You think innovatively, creatively, and out of the box.

This means:

- *You see past the end of your nose: from the directly visible wishes and needs of people or organizations, you derive the underlying needs or expectations.*
- *Stepping out of the box, you design creative and innovative alternative ways to meet these underlying needs.*
- *For each of these alternatives, you discover the main consequences, and you weigh them against each other.*
- *Based on your conclusions, you arrive at innovative and at the same time realistic recommendations, decisions, or actions.*

As I mentioned earlier, according to the Brundtland Report, sustainable development is:

> *"a development that meets the needs of the present without compromising the ability of future generations to meet their own needs."*

Apparently sustainability is about fulfilling needs and the ability to continue doing so in the future. This raises a fundamental question: *which* needs?

Is a second car for everyone such a need? How about a second home and a yacht in the harbor? What about exotic foods flown in by plane? Clearly everything is not feasible; what our planet can offer us has limits. Therefore, if we want to advance sustainability, it is important to discuss the kinds of needs we have.

A clever tool for this is Maslow's well-known hierarchy of needs pyramid, which distinguishes five levels of needs – from basic needs such as food and oxygen up to more psychological needs like esteem and self-actualization. For example, imagine you would like to drink a cup of coffee. Why, actually? Which need to you want to fulfill? Are you thirsty? (physiological need, Level 1 of Maslow's pyramid). Would you like to hold something in your hands? (safety need, Maslow's Level 2). Or do you feel a need for coziness and human interaction? (love and belonging, Maslow's Level 3). In other words, which *function* does the cup of java have to serve?

The example of the cup of coffee shows that what constitutes a need defies simple definitions because appearances can be deceiving. In many cases, the expressed needs differ from the real ones. Often people have a feeling that they would want to satisfy a certain need, while in reality – perhaps without being aware of it – they cherish some other deeply-rooted need. The function of a cup of coffee, a good conversation, a diploma, a partner for life, a job, a private business, or a car is in many cases not the one you might think of at first sight. What is the underlying function, *the need behind the need*? Could it be a need you aren't even conscious of?

Every professional has the task to fulfill needs. Check it out! Doctors and nurses fulfill patients' needs for improved health. Researchers and teachers fulfill needs for knowledge; managers the need for guidance, control, or support; producers and shop owners the need for products; consultants the need for advice; and so forth. Which needs do you fulfill, and for whom?

Now, as a professional, you can simply do what you are asked to, but you might also think critically about your task and initiate your own changes or additions. This book is filled with beautiful examples. One way to begin is to think deeply about which needs you really are fulfilling. Think about *the need behind the need*. If you do this, you start thinking out of the box, and you embrace wild creativity and splendid innovations. You give yourself the opportunity to find totally new ways to fulfill human needs now and in the future.

A fine method to discover needs behind needs is a "function analysis." When you apply this method, you return mentally to your early childhood – when you were about two or three years old – to the "why" phase. In short, whenever a need is mentioned, you are going to ask "Why?"

Look at a concrete example.

When someone tells you: You ask:

1   *I want to buy a refrigerator!*   *Why?*
2   *Because I want to have a refrigerator in my house!*   *Why?*
3   *Because I want to keep my food cool!*   *Why?*
4   *Because I want to store food in my house!*   *Why?*
5   *Because I want to have my favorite food available*
    at any time!   *Why?*
6   *Because I want to have pleasure without limits!*   *Why?*
7   *Because I . . . (etc.)*

The fun thing is that each subsequent step opens up a pathway to alternative solutions to fulfill the need.

Statement #1 has just one solution: just buy it, this fridge!

Statement #2 allows for alternatives because you could also try to lease a refrigerator – that fits nicely with the notion of a circular economy – or you could borrow one, or share one with your neighbors or even the whole village. (Steal it?)

Statement #3 offers even more options. Cooling can also be done in a basement, though this may not be suitable for ice cream, I admit.

Statement #4 is about conserving food. However, cooling is not the only option. Instead you can bottle it, can it, freeze-dry it, radiate it, marinate or pickle it (although radiation and salt are not very popular these days) and much more. In short, this statement renders many new alternatives, and so does Statement #5. If you wish to have food available at any time, why not use a delivery service, or how about a pipe structure from the supermarket to your house? One – two – three, and the fresh spinach, harvested half an hour ago, pops out of the hatch!

About Statement #6, pleasure without limits can be had in many ways: playing sports, watching TV, having sex, or installing a new app on your smartphone. Eating is not the only way to have fun!

I did not fill in Statement #7. If I had, there's a big chance that the discussion would have moved to philosophical issues, perhaps even to the meaning of life. Wonderful, isn't it?

Function analysis is tremendously important for sustainable development. If you don't do it and just immediately respond to every desire (see Statement #1), there's a good chance that we will all end up in a world dominated by even more excessive materialistic consumerism, in which every need is directly translated into a shiny industrial product or a neatly performed, costly service: a facelift, a holiday trip to the Bahamas, you name it. Not only will the financial cost be tremendous, but also from a sustainability angle, this will not be feasible at all. That is why it is so important to search systematically for the needs behind the needs – to ask further. Then, instead of just having one answer to the expressed need, you will get a whole range of possible answers to choose from. This is all the more true if you find innovative alternatives instead of treading down the same old paths. Such a creative way of thinking will enable you to discover the most sustainable way to achieve what Brundtland asks: fulfill the needs of people in the present and in the future.

For the future of a business, function analysis also presents a great instrument. Do you remember the entrepreneur who, at the beginning of the chapter, was convinced that *of course* his company would still exist in twenty years because it delivers excellent products or services? If every now and then this entrepreneur, preferably together with some independent and creative outsiders, took the time to think about the question of whether his products or services will still be popular within the society of the future, he would gain new insights into the opportunities and threats concerning the continuity of his company. If his chances are low, it may be necessary to redefine the company's mission, for instance, quit selling refrigerators and instead start leasing them.

CHAPTER NINE

The toolbox of the professional

In Chapter 3, I wrote about competences and told you the following:

> A **competence** is the ability to deliver, in a given **context**, in a certain role, solid **achievements** making use of appropriate **tools**.

You may have noticed in Chapters 2, 4, 6, etc., that every competence was described as a set of three achievements that are delivered. But how about the appropriate tools?

In many cases, the tools of professionals are tangible such as hammers, pipe wrenches, or computers. Other tools are in your head, for instance, people skills, or architectural insight. There are four kinds of such "mental" tools. Together, they are referred to as "KISA," an acronym that stands for:

Knowledge	*= what you know*
Insight	*= what you understand*
Skills	*= what you are able to do*
Attitude	*= who you are*

For the competences that have been dealt with so far, a lot of these tools have been mentioned. I will present you with a brief overview.

Knowledge:

The concept "consequence scope" and "consequence period" (R1, Chapter 2)

The *Triple P*: people, planet, profit (S2, Chapter 6)

Linear and non-linear processes (F2, Chapter 8)

Maslow's hierarchy of needs (F3, Chapter 8)

Insight:

You distinguish between facts, assumptions, and opinions (E2, Chapter 4)

You position the system within its context (S1, Chapter 6)

You recognize flaws in the fabric and sources of vigor (S2, Chapter 6)

You understand the difference between tackling symptoms and removing causes (F1, Chapter 8)

Skills:

Create a stakeholder analysis (R1, Chapter 2)

Listen actively (E1, Chapter 4)

Cooperate in interdisciplinary and transdisciplinary ways (E3, Chapter 4)

Perform a function analysis (F3, Chapter 8)

Attitude:

You feel and show personal responsibility (R2, Chapter 2)

You respect values (E1, Chapter 4)

You think and act integrally and chain-oriented (S3, Chapter 6)

You think innovatively, creatively, and out of the box (F3, Chapter 8)

If you have all these tools in your repertoire, you possess a well-equipped toolbox to work sustainably. This is also true for the tools of the next two competences, which will be described in the coming chapters (10 and 12), especially the first one in Chapter 10, which deals with your personal attitude.

CHAPTER TEN
Involvement

The Competence (Figure 10.1):

A sustainably competent professional has a personal involvement in sustainable development.

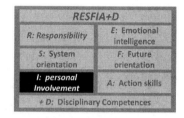

Figure 10.1 *Competence I: personal Involvement*

Attitude = who you are, I wrote in the last chapter. Then, who are you as a person? At the beginning of the book, I told you that most people fulfill three roles during their lifetime. Together these roles form a kind of triangle: the citizen, the consumer, and the professional. This book is primarily about the third role, the sustainably competent professional. But *are* you that professional, or do you just play that role? That is the topic of this chapter.

People who, as professionals, have a strong influence on sustainability share a number of characteristics. This is true for all the "heroes" who tell their stories in this book. They have a *passion* for what they do, and they pursue it wholeheartedly. They don't just act sustainably. They live and breathe it. It's what they identify with and what they exist for. As their three roles as citizen, consumer, and professional merge, they coalesce into "real" and "whole" individuals who intensely experience sustainability or selected aspects of it. For these people, their profession is also their hobby and their passion. When I meet people like that, it's always wonderful to see them. Do you know such individuals? Maybe you are one of them. Maybe you are on your way to becoming a person like that.

In this chapter, I will focus on three achievements delivered by such people:

- *Consistently involve sustainable development in his or her own work as a professional (sustainable attitude)*
- *Passionately work toward dreams and ideals*
- *Employ his or her conscience as the ultimate yardstick*

10.1 SUSTAINABLE ATTITUDE

For John Jordan, a young social entrepreneur from Maryland, sustainability is more than an idea: "It's a lifestyle," he is convinced. A graduate of Morehouse College, where he studied finance, leadership, and economics, John first became involved in social entrepreneurship when he built a student character development curriculum. "That's when I discovered that people have the ability to change the institutions that they are part of," he says. An activist was born!

"When I was in seventh grade, my dad lost his third-generation roofing company due to his poor health." John remembers. "He had high blood pressure and diabetes and suffered two strokes as a result of poor eating habits. Inside of this loss is where we really built our bond. In America, you go to college to gain a skill and a way of thinking, but I also always knew that I wanted to be an entrepreneur like my dad because it would give me the freedom that my mom, who worked in Corporate America, never had."

While John was still in college, a unique opportunity emerged. "I won an Oprah Winfrey South African Fellowship, which led me to understand how the same sustainability issues that existed in black communities in the US were present in communities around historically black universities in South Africa." Now John applies the lessons he learned about global sustainable development in his work for a non-governmental organization called Fight for Light. "We collaborate with anchor institutions, local organizations, and community members across the US to transform and develop sustainable communities."

John's sustainable attitude is tangible. Phrases like "collaborative innovation," "collective thinking," and "collective imagination" just roll off his tongue.

"Basically, we bring existing organization together and connect them with other local citizens who care about the same issues such as social justice and environmental protection – breaking down silos or false borders. For example, at the University of Colorado Boulder, you have the sustainability group at the Environmental Center and the Student Outreach and Retention Center for Equity (SORCE). The Environmental Center group never talks to the students of color, and the folks from SORCE don't engage with sustainability initiatives. So Fight for Light facilitates an engagement between the two and sort of 'translates' for them, using a sustainability framework that works for both parties," explains John.

"When you're looking at community development," he adds, "the number one reason communities are often unsustainable is because the ideas and development plans did not originate from the actual people who *live* in that place and *know* that place. Developers, for example, lured by special tax credits and incentives, come to these neighborhoods and build developments, products, and services that aren't needed. The community does not own the economic value that gets created. In Martin Luther King's old neighborhood, the Old Fourth Ward, a historic neighborhood in Atlanta, for instance, a high percentage of residents had to move out of the city as a result of development. They simply could not afford to live there anymore. Most of the developers who made money were external or from Buckhead, a predominately white district of Atlanta."

In order to solve this kind of problem, John and his teammates facilitate collaborative innovation workshops that bring together the ideas of sustainability and social equity to create new social innovations. Their training empowers students and participants with knowledge and skills to advance sustainability and social justice efforts.

"To improve these causes of unsustainability," John goes on to explain, "I help leverage existing capital and infrastructure of anchor institutions – colleges and universities, hospitals, schools, and churches connected to that place – to realize the collective imagination that Fight for Light inspires and orchestrates. We connect the resources of a university, for instance, with local organizations and corporations that work on sustainability issues such as energy conservation, healthcare, education, and transportation. In Colorado, we worked with the director of the Environmental Center at CU Boulder and their student government association's budget to pay for the Eco-Social Justice Leadership program that SORCE and the Environmental Center students collectively imagined in their innovation workshop. This funding also covers annual community convening and student trainings across Boulder, Longmont, Lafayette, and the Denver metro area to build alliances, fund environmental justice related research and to underwrite new programming. This conference is the center point for collaboration across the area that would never have existed without this eco-social justice lens!"

According to John, the key is "to really match the local need with the local resource. That resource often comes from reimagining or retooling that which already exists. When I meet with stakeholders, I emphasize the possibilities of an interactive experience, and I communicate the successes of these sustainable social innovation projects. I use stories that resonate with people and that help them envision new possibilities." We need more storytellers like John.

THE ACHIEVEMENT

You involve sustainable development consistently in your work as a professional. You have a sustainable attitude.

This means:

- *You know what sustainable development is, and you explain the concept to others.*
- *In practical situations, you name causes of unsustainability in and around your work.*
- *You design methods to improve these causes of unsustainability, and you introduce them in a constructive way to your colleagues, executives, and/or employees.*
- *For you this is obviously "second nature," and you do it consistently.*

10.2 PASSIONS, DREAMS, AND IDEALS

Every now and then, I get an email or a phone call from *Speakers Academy* inquiring whether I would be available to give a presentation somewhere. This happened again a few months ago and involved a request by three students who were organizing a symposium for their university. The symposium was called "Sustism," an abbreviation of "Sustainable Tourism." "Unfortunately," *Speakers Academy* informed me, "they don't have a budget. Nevertheless, if you are interested in speaking there, feel free to contact them."

I have a soft spot for students: not much money, lots of idealism, ambition, and potential for growth. So, I decided to do the presentation. I hope you don't mind if I borrow one of the stories in this book from my own work.

On the day of the "Sustism" symposium, I had 45 minutes for my presentation. About 200 students filed into the auditorium. A bit giggly and noisy, they found their seats, and the host who was about to introduce me had some trouble getting them to settle down. Not a big surprise, as the audience had already sat through three 45-minute lectures – without a break: a beginner's mistake of the organizers perhaps?

I started with some jokes and BIG WORDS: "Look how *magnificent* it is," I exclaimed, drawing large gestures with my arms to underscore the indeed marvelous photograph of our planet Earth as captured by NASA. "I am so proud to be living here! Yes, you are too. I know!" This drew their attention. A bit later, I showed them a picture taken on the island of Java and invited the listeners to tell me what they saw. The answers came from all corners of the lecture hall: "A garbage dump!" "A slum!"

Yes, both answers were correct since the photo depicted a huge collection of slum dwellings built on stakes above a garbage dump. "And the water?" I asked. The audience came to the conclusion that the river on the photograph was at once an open sewer for a city upstream and the bathing, cooking, and drinking water of the slum dwellers. "Imagine,"

I said. "This is the place where these people live their lives, where their *children* are born, and where those same kids, a couple of years later, play with the filth they find in the garbage." It was absolutely quiet in the lecture hall now, and I continued almost whispering (with a microphone, all right): "These people don't belong anywhere. They have been cast out from society; nobody wants them."

I outlined some additional sustainability problems, ranging from climate change to violations of human rights, which are embedded as "weaving faults" in the systems humans build. Then I arranged them in a scheme that showed how all these problems were interconnected. "You simply cannot take these weaving faults one by one and solve them separately," I explained. "You have to address them together, however complicated it may be."

On the screen, the following message appeared:

Complex problems
demand
complex solutions.
Therefore, we need
massive numbers of people
who contribute.

I described how people, taken as a group and as individuals, are essentially sources of vigor that can help us eradicate weaving faults. As I described in Chapter 6, other sources of vigor are, for example, inspiring ideas and texts, science and technology, and nature. Yet others include governments, businesses, NGOs, and schools. "In order to tackle the weaving faults, we just need every professional," I told the audience, "especially those with a proper education, like you." Then I added, with extra emphasis: "You are essential!" It seemed to take a while before the audience started breathing again.

Every single time, I am thrilled about reaching an audience on an emotional level. Twenty years ago I used my presentations primarily to transmit information. My slide shows contained a lot of text back then.

Nowadays, I still convey information, of course, but my focus is on the experience, and this works fabulously.

In my presentation at this particular university, I introduced sustainable development as a sort of competition between the sources of vigor and the weaving faults. "Sources of vigor against weaving faults; if it were a soccer match, what would be the score: 1–0 perhaps, or 0–1? Well, the facts compel me to admit that presently we, the sources of vigor, are behind. The combined global ecological footprint is about 1.4 times higher than the carrying capacity (the biocapacity) of the Earth, which is simply not acceptable. Luckily, it does not have to stay that way! If everyone contributes, we can bend the score in our favor. In that case, we not only make the world a lot more sustainable, but we also create a far more beautiful version of it." Then I added: "It's simply a matter of wanting it."

Dear reader, I have a request. Do you have any ideals? For a better world, a better life, your own personal developments, whatever? Hold on to them; don't relinquish them. If you are concerned about making those ideals come true, you will, of course, have to be ready to compromise. Not every ideal can be fully realized since you cannot completely manipulate reality according to your wishes. So, adjust your goals, or else you will probably achieve next to nothing. However, don't give up on your actual ideals. Preserve them and cherish them. They belong to the most precious things you possess.

THE ACHIEVEMENT

You passionately work toward your dreams and ideals.

This means:

- *You describe the wishes, dreams, and ideals you cherish regarding the work that you do and the results and effects of it.*
- *You openly express these dreams and ideals within your direct working environment.*
- *You state your professional dreams and ideals in your expressed goals and in the implementation of your work.*

- *Thus you inspire others in your working environment: colleagues, superiors, and/or employees.*
- *Your dreams and ideas lead to original, innovative ideas and projects related to your professional activities, work environment, discipline, or line of business.*

10.3 CONSCIENCE

"I drove to the office, handed in my car keys, the keys to the stores, my cell phone, and then I quit." That is what Jenny Parren wrote to me, and in her lines you can still sense the tension the incident caused.

Jenny was employed in a well-known clothing chain. She had risen from salesclerk to store manager to regional manager. She did very well until the board appointed a new director as a supervisor to the regional managers. "Let me call her Josie," Jenny writes.

Soon the atmosphere in the company started changing. Josie appeared to be a tough businesswoman, and she dragged the board into her new way of doing things as well. The enterprise became more business-like, increasingly aiming at short-term financial gains. Jenny had to work very hard, up to 60 hours a week, but was paid only for 40 hours. Even worse, Jenny was forced to demand the same from the store employees. On most days, they had to continue working for at least an hour after the stores closed, without being paid overtime.

Jenny tried to improve the situation, but a meeting with the board, comprised of the owners of the company, led to nothing. It appeared as though the board members trusted Josie completely, and that was that.

Shortly before Christmas, the situation escalated. "One of my salesgirls was sick while working in the store," Parren writes. "She suffered from a bad flu, so I sent her home on Monday as she was seriously ill. When Josie heard this, she demanded the girl be fired when she returned. The girl had been scheduled to get a full-time position right after Christmas, but according to Josie, someone who became ill just before Christmas could not be trusted and wasn't worth being offered a permanent position."

For Jenny, this was unacceptable. "It put me in conflict with my own norms and values. If I let her go, I would never be able to look at myself in the mirror." She refused to fire her staff member. As a reaction, Josie waited until Jenny had a day off and fired the staff member herself.

This was too much for Jenny. She immediately handed in her resignation. Josie attempted to respect her term of notice, but Jenny gave her no real choice: her resignation was to be accepted immediately, or else she would call in sick due to overstrain. Josie made the best of it and accepted Jenny's immediate resignation.

Two days later, Jenny had a new job. Later, she decided to continue her academic education in cultural and social coaching, which she had given up to work in the clothing business. Jenny graduated and now coaches 17–23 year-olds who want to contribute to the livability of their local communities.

THE ACHIEVEMENT

You employ your own conscience as the ultimate yardstick.

This means:

- *You investigate the goals, methods, tasks, and assignments of your professional activities based on your own values and ethical standards. You define the results of this investigation for yourself.*
- *You either do not accept or perform goals, assignments, or activities conflicting with your values, or you modify them until they agree with your conscience.*
- *You remain firm in your decisions, and you formulate them in an assertive yet courteous manner. Although you are open to reasonable arguments of others, you are not susceptible to their pressure.*
- *In your work, you exhibit exemplary behavior and leadership thanks to your openly conscientious approach.*

"If it really matters, conscience comes before the law." That's what I said a couple of years ago to someone I was talking to. In my view, this was self-evident, but to my surprise, the woman I spoke with reacted by asking:

"Really? I think it's the other way around."

This was the start of a fascinating discussion. She asserted:

"It would be a mess if people started deciding all by themselves what is ethically right!"

"Just the opposite," I responded. "If people shut off their conscience and blindly obey the laws or what the government demands, then it will be a mess. '*Befehl ist Befehl!*' (German for 'orders are orders'), have you ever heard of that? That's how wars are caused – and holocausts. Please let everyone think for himself!"

"Oh, yes!" she scorned. "So, you think it's okay when every fraudster judges everything by himself, that it's no problem if he is cheating people or companies?"

"Well no, I . . ."

"Or if rapists think that women were only asking for it?"

"Now you're getting . . ."

"And what about terrorists who take out their anger and frustration on innocent people?"

"No, that's not at all what I am trying to say!" I quickly added. "Listen, I don't claim people can freely choose between the law and their wallet, or between the law and their lower lust, or – considering those terrorists – between the law and their personal aggression. But people can definitely choose between the law and their conscience. I'm talking about a fair and conscientious consideration, not just in any futile case, of course, and not just on any day if it happens to come in handy. Only in exceptional circumstances: if you feel others are forcing you to do things – or not to do them – and you feel with all your heart and soul that it isn't right."

"Well, I think it's extremely dangerous!" she insisted.

"It is," I admitted, "but the opposite – slavish obedience to the authorities – is even more dangerous."

I don't think she was convinced, but I was. How about you? In my opinion, your own conscience should be the ultimate yardstick for what is right – not the laws, the regulations at your work, or the orders or desires of your managers or clients. Different people will apply different norms and ethical rules, of course. That's how it should be. In our society, in which personal freedom is considered highly important, this will only work if it is complemented by personal responsibility of citizens, consumers, and professionals. Hence, my proposition: a sustainably competent professional employs his or her own conscience as the ultimate yardstick.

CHAPTER ELEVEN

Every profession has its own competences

In Chapters 2, 4, 6, 8, 10, and 12, I tell the stories of people who have shown that they possess competences you would like to see in all professionals regardless of their education or expertise, their profession or discipline, or the level at which they work. In addition, there are all kinds of sustainability competences that differ for each profession. Every job requires its own special skills. The present chapter is dedicated to such disciplinary competences as I announced at the beginning of Chapter 2; see Figure 11.1.

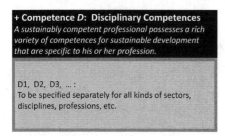
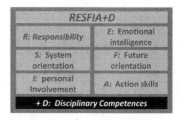

Figure 11.1 +*Competence D: Disciplinary competences*

A complete enumeration of all disciplinary sustainability competences is impossible. Thousands of different professions and disciplines exist, each with its own specific needs for expertise and experiences. So, I have selected a limited number of professions. For each of them, I present one or more examples of roles that may be fulfilled and of achievements that may be delivered to contribute to sustainable development. In a number of cases, this will be about social sustainability, in others about economic or ecological sustainability. Together, the stories will form a colorful collection showing in a kaleidoscopic way a range of aspects belonging to professionals who contribute to sustainability.

THE MANAGER

Context:
Be Green Packaging

Role:
Director of Eco-Social Initiatives

Achievement:

Making an impact by educating consumers and businesses on sustainable packaging and helping to create a zero-waste facility

As a sophomore at UC–Santa Barbara, Eva Van Wingerden first read *Cradle to Cradle*, the seminal work on regenerative product design by William McDonough and Michael Braungart. Eva was not yet thinking about what career she wanted to pursue. She just loved learning about the environment and the ways human beings could impact it, she says. "That's when the reality dawned on me that every action and every choice we make has an impact on not just our immediate surroundings, but on the entire global environment. It was a very profound realization for me."

For the past three and a half years, Eva has been working as Director of Eco-Social Initiatives for Be Green Packaging in California. She manages the environmental certifications, plays an active role in product testing, quality control, and facility audits, and also does consulting. She enjoys telling the story of how Be Green Packaging got started. One of the company's original founders, Ron Blitzer, had been in the drinking straw business, she recounts. "One day, fulfilling his duties as a true Southern Californian, Blitzer noticed all of the plastic debris floating around him. He realized that he wanted to be part of the solution rather than a contributor to the problem. The idea of Be Green Packaging was born."

Be Green Packaging, whose corporate clients include Whole Foods Market and Gillette, produces sustainable consumer and food packaging that is Cradle to Cradle Certified™. The raw materials, Eva explains, are sourced from different vendors who are vetted by the supply chain team to ensure they meet the company's standards and certification requirements. "Our products are designed to be single use and are tested (under ASTM standards) and certified to be compostable in industrial composting facilities. We have even heard from a few customers that they have successfully composted our products in their backyard compost."

"Convenience is king," Eva notes, "but people want to do the right thing. In a perfect world, everything would be reusable, and we wouldn't need single use packaging. But it seems that we have a long way to go to reach that paradigm. In the meantime, Be Green Packaging's compostable fiber products are a step on the road to a perfect world. Our manufacturing process produces little to no material that is not compostable, recyclable, or reusable. Our products offer the option for people to use a package that is convenient, single use, made from rapidly renewable fibers, and ends up in a continuous biological nutrient cycle."

That sounds nearly perfect, but as mentioned in Chapter 6, when it comes to moving toward a circular economy, reality is often more complicated. In fact, Eva finds that educating customers about where the product goes once they are finished using it poses a challenge: "The useful life cycle of our products can be anywhere from say 15 minutes to a day or two. It is a complete waste of useful material to let these products sit in a landfill for hundreds of years in an anaerobic museum of garbage. Instead, why not avoid wasting the product and filling up our landfills by throwing it in the compost? However, if it is not easy and accessible, people will not and cannot make composting part of their thought process. Habits take a lot of time and conscious effort to change, so the easier we make it, the more people will do it."

So how can a manager like her make an impact? Eva thinks that her biggest achievement has been working toward turning the company's new domestic manufacturing plant in South Carolina into a zero waste facility. "It's still a work in progress," she cautions. The hurdles range from low tipping fees (a charge hauling facilities must pay to dispose of garbage in landfills), to lack of education and employee training about waste diversion, to non-existent industrial composting facilities, she explains. "Our team has been implementing single stream recycling, collection for special materials, composting on site, and we have even built community gardens where local students come and learn about gardening and composting and get their hands dirty. Getting involved with the local community and educating young people about environmental impact and composting is my favorite part about what I do at Be Green."

As a young professional, Eva believes it is vital to enjoy the subject matter, ask questions, and get involved. "In academia and especially in environmental professions," she says, "it can be easy to see the negative and get bewildered and overwhelmed with all the problems and the ways that human beings contribute to environmental degradation . . . I find that I am most positively effective when I am hopeful about the impact I can make. I try to read articles about people doing positive things for each other or inventing products that improve efficiency and minimize environmental effects and waste. All of these things help remind me that every choice I make can have meaningful impact."

THE FINANCIAL ADVISOR

Context:
Vancity

Role:
Guardian of the balance between people, planet, and profit

Achievement:
Advising businesses on how to balance their sustainable vision and financial goals

Brian Cade started working for Vancity, a values-based financial cooperative in Vancouver, Canada, fresh out of university ten years ago. The banking cooperative, a member of the Global Alliance for Banking on Values, adheres to the triple bottom line, putting "people before profit." After reading on Vancity's website that the cooperative not only seeks "the opportunity to work with organizations that are also taking significant steps to improve their social, ethical, and environmental performance," but that it also had a reputation for being a "great employer," Cade applied and gradually worked his way up to his current position as account manager in the community business division. His duties are evaluating loan requests and advising entrepreneurs.

"We evaluate requests not only based on the cash flow of the applicant," Cade explains. "We take other factors into consideration when assessing the risk of lending. We also look at the potential community benefits of the business and the strength of the people behind it, their team."

"When we work with non-profit organizations," Brian continues, "it often means that we are willing to take different risks and be more creative, recognizing that a non-profit's success looks different. Their goal isn't profit. Any organization that's operating differently than their competitors because they are, for example, more socially and environmentally progressive, needs to be evaluated based on that added value." An example of social impact, he explains, could be offering living wages or employing individuals with mental disabilities. It could also be a business that demonstrates cooperative principles by supporting similar businesses in the community to grow and overcome barriers to entry. "In a capitalist sense, this is counterintuitive," says Cade, "but ultimately it creates a more robust local economy and better community. From a risk perspective, these organizations may have more cash flow challenges early on but will actually be more competitive in the future as they are recognized as an industry leader. We have to factor all of this into our own credit adjudication."

"For instance, there is a commercial organic waste disposal business that we've worked with for several years since their start up," Cade adds. "They've had good press because they were one of the first companies offering office kitchen composting . . . making a positive environmental impact in the community by diverting organic waste from the landfill. They continually came to us seeking financing for their anticipated growth. We spent many coaching sessions testing their projections and helping them to better manage their growth and their capacity for debt. We are pleased that they have been able to weather the slow years and manage fluctuating gross profit margins. Had the company leveraged too heavily in the early years, they would have been unable to manage their cash flow, causing the business to falter on client contracts or debt repayment."

"We also have to consider where industries are moving and what is considered common practice. For example, years ago it was innovative and challenging for restaurants to source any of their food from local suppliers. A commitment to do this would be considered significant. Today, this is more common and very much on trend, so we tend to look for companies to not just make the effort to buy local, but to fully commit to specific suppliers. For local producers, having consistent and reliable orders from customers is a huge advantage as they are often planting vegetables or raising livestock well in advance. Ultimately this helps to stabilize our local food economy."

When Brian and his friends who work at traditional banks and accounting firms get together to talk shop and share stories, he notices a difference: "They're often just judged on an hourly basis based on profitability. In contrast, we get to seek out people who want to make a difference in their community, and we're given the extra time to get to know the client. We are allowed a longer time horizon to build and maintain an open relationship with the client and become a trusted advisor. A lot of these early-stage businesses need to be given more of a benefit of the doubt. We look at their sustainability mission and community impact and don't force them into a box."

To those just starting out in the field of banking, Brian suggests, "Bring your passion to your careers as it can be contagious to those around you. Don't underestimate the power of small wins when working with organizations that are making positive social and environmental contributions. You'll be surprised how quickly these incremental steps forward amount to big changes in the industry and your community."

THE ARTIST

Context:

Teo Castellanos, actor/writer/director/educator

Role:

Conscience of society

Achievement:

Wake up, protest, put into perspective, involve, start dialogue, bring peace, entertain, inspire action, and make people laugh

We hear Haitian kompa music as Jitney driver argues with passenger in Kreyol. Stops to pick up another passenger (tourist)

Jitney driver: (To tourist) Yes, where you go? Design . . . Design Distwict? Whas dat? . . . I go stwait Northeast Second Avenue. OK come, sit in fwont I take you. Come one dolla . . . one dolla . . . Where you go? . . . Gallewie? . . . OK I know come. Come. (To argumentative passenger) Shut up! No I don turn off ma mizik. You don't lak ma mizik? . . . get off, tek slowbus!

"With *NE 2nd Avenue (2003)*, where I play all nine characters, I wanted to give a slice of Miami and some of the issues we face here to the world. I also wanted to introduce us to *ourselves* to bridge cultural gaps. We live in a multicultural city; yet, we often don't know each other. After one show, a Cuban man came up to me and said: 'I loved the play but I didn't understand a single word the Jamaican guy said.' Well, I try to be authentic with the speech patterns while keeping it understandable, so I told him he needed to hang out at a Jamaican spot."

Over vegetarian Thai curry, Teo Castellanos reflects on his role as 'conscience' of contemporary US society. Born in Puerto Rico, but raised in the United States, the bilingual artist understands all too well that culture is fluid and prevailing thought patterns challenge our ideas of ethical behavior. "I wanted to represent my city and to find a commonality." When I took *NE 2nd Avenue* to Europe, people were wondering how the show would be received, but they got it – even if they didn't understand every word or nuance." The play won the First Award at the Edinburgh Festival Fringe in 2003, a sign that the play's message was universal.

"The biggest challenge for any activist is changing thought patterns," Castellanos believes. "*Scratch & Burn* (2005) is a pro-peace ritual influenced by hip-hop and a response to the US invasion of Iraq. It criticizes the government and the military industrial complex, but the majority of people in the audience were opposed to the war themselves. *Scratch & Burn* was received very well. Everyone was happy, but it was like preaching to the choir."

On the other hand, *Fat Boy*, Castellanos' dance theater play, which premiered in 2010, pointed a finger at the audience. "On a broad level, it addresses American waste and consumerism juxtaposed by world hunger and poverty," Castellanos explains. "*Fat Boy* is a reflection on society, yes, *and* the individual." The play deals with greed and over-consumption, but as Castellanos sees it, "Greed is really the fear of not having enough, so it made you reflect a little." While audiences had embraced the director's earlier productions, some people "didn't get quite behind it (*Fat Boy*)." Castellanos: "I put a mirror to society, asking people to look at their own behavior and confront any disconnect between their opinions and actions. Suddenly, people had to ponder their own consumption patterns and wonder, 'Am I afraid of donating – of sharing my resources?'"

Makyo: You know it's a Black Friday when you get trampled to death by sheep consumed by consumption, real bullets fly in stores with toy guns and camping is done on the concrete of Best Buy sidewalks. (*Fat Boy*)

Castellanos' art is informed by his spiritual practice – Zen Buddhism. His perspective comes from "turning to ourselves and looking at someone with compassion instead of blame." He feels that it is important to model ethical behavior, so he partnered with a food bank to donate parts of the proceeds of *Fat Boy* from CD sales. He eats a plant-based diet because he objects to factory farming and believes in non-violence. He also chooses to eat a meatless diet because it promotes sustainability by conserving resources. This is *his* conscience at work.

As an artist and activist, Castellanos always seeks to inspire through his actions. He is passionate about public transportation in urban areas, an issue that has come to the forefront in many American cities precisely because they are so congested and often lack adequate public alternatives to driving a car. "Again, to change people's way of thinking is difficult," Castellanos says, so to commute to a movement class he teaches at an arts college, he rides his bicycle to show that he's doing it and "sharing that with people." Even though he owns an economical Fiat, he also takes local buses, trains, and skateboards, and believes that it is vital to support the people in the community – "the train conductors and bus drivers." After all, they inspire the characters in his plays:

Jitney driver: "My kids, my kids don lak my mizik. I have a pwobwem wid my kids; dey speak vewy good English. I don speak English so good, so dey twy to twick me. My son, my son bwing home his weport card, he tell me "F" on his weport card mean Fabulous!" (*NE 2nd Ave*)

What keeps Castellanos inspired? "Working with young people," he says. He has coached spoken word teams with local youths for several years. The performance-based poems explore a range of social justice conflicts and controversial topics such as human trafficking, child soldiers, immigration, gun violence, lost languages, as well as works addressing the "Black Lives Matter" movement.

Recently Castellanos developed and directed "Conscience Under Fire," a set of spoken word pieces written by The Combat Hippies, four Iraq War veterans, who also perform in the play. The show, which deals with the mental wounds inflicted by combat and post-traumatic stress,

EVERY PROFESSION HAS ITS OWN CONSEQUENCES

was performed on September 11, an auspicious date for any American audience. Castellanos hopes that his works will wake people up, inspire action, and ultimately bring about healing and peace.

THE ENVIRONMENTAL MANAGER

Context:
EY (Ernst & Young)

Role:
Sustainability strategy developer balancing the Triple Bottom Line pillars

Achievement:
Implement an environmental strategy that addresses people, planet, and profits

Are you looking for a great way to start a conversation about the importance of sustainability? Try green nail polish! According to Leisha John, Americas Director of Environmental Sustainability for EY, it works. Many of the people she encounters remark about her polish, providing her the opportunity to explain what the color represents and why we need to address the issue of sustainability.

Thirty years ago, when Leisha John first began working for EY, financial advisors were not concerned with including environmental sustainability information and metrics in their annual reports. Now, things have changed. Today's leading companies voluntarily report on their environmental impacts, and not only that. When clients send requests for proposals, they also want to know how the professional services firms they engage are reducing their own carbon footprint. This is where Leisha comes in.

As one of the four largest global professional services firms, EY employs 210,000 people worldwide. All these employees work in temperature controlled spaces, turn on lights, use computers, print reports, use lavatories, eat in the cafeteria, drink coffee, and travel around the globe to meet with their clients and with each other. This presents a "great opportunity for operational greening," Leisha asserts. By encouraging telecommuting and telepresence, a sophisticated form of videoconferencing, the company has been able to reduce its non-essential business travel. And by leasing greener space and using space more efficiently, EY is able to better control real estate spending and lower its energy bills. Leisha, a Certified Public Accountant (CPA), herself works from her home office.

"Retrofitting existing spaces with energy-saving devices provides another way to save money and the environment," Leisha notes. She goes on to describe the potential energy savings from converting all light fixtures to LEDs in an entire building in New York City. "Waste stream reductions are also crucial: reducing disposable coffee cups saves resources; going tray-free in the cafeteria reduces food waste while saving gallons of water otherwise used to rinse trays; and introducing swipe-card technology encourages mindful printing and copying, resulting in fewer trees being cut and reducing toner usage too."

The impact of international travel on the climate and how much carbon and money can be saved when video conferencing replaces travel is also compelling. "Reducing CO_2 increases the bottom line. Carbon savings and dollar savings generally go hand-in-hand," Leisha stresses. "And if we can provide green alternatives to business travel, we can save our clients and our firm money while simultaneously reducing our carbon emissions."

In today's competitive global economy, companies feel a lot of pressure in terms of "brand and reputational risk" when they see "others going green," the sustainability executive says. "If a firm wants to attract the best talent and convince clients to use its services, it has to emphasize sustainability values and demonstrate how the organization 'walks the talk'. Likewise, clients demand transparency regarding the environmental and social impact of the operations of their suppliers."

Leisha John is making sure that EY can model corporate responsibility and accountability by reaching out to its stakeholders to determine what they think is most material and relevant for EY to address. EY's nearly a quarter of a million employees, the firm's global clients, the vendors whose increasingly sustainable products EY procures, and the communities in cities around the world where EY operates: All of them play a role in helping EY reduce its environmental impact and in being transparent in reporting its progress. "And because EY also offers 'Climate Change and Sustainability Services' to clients, it's crucial that the firm 'walks the talk' in order to be credible in the market," Leisha John adds.

When asked about challenges, Leisha John replies that some aspects are easier than others: "Firm wide operational improvements (e.g., print management systems that require a badge swipe) are easier to implement". But often it is much harder to alter "the little things like getting employees to green their own behaviors." For example, when it comes to throwing recyclables into the correct bin or adjusting to a more sustainable plants-based diet, it is difficult to get people to rethink their habits. To get the results you are aiming for, you have to "know your audience," Leisha believes.

Leisha shares her passion for sustainability in her TEDx Talk, where she reveals that green is not her only favorite color. She also champions the color white, especially when it comes in the form of white coating that can turn a dark roof into a solar-reflecting and energy-saving asset: "White roofs for green schools" she calls this "simple, cheap, and doable solution," adding that the rebates given by utility companies can cover the cost of coating roofs white. If applied on every school's roofs, it could save the nation's school districts millions of dollars, savings that could then go toward funding school programs, technology upgrades, and teacher salaries. To help her spread the idea "from Georgia, to Texas, to California," she created a website. Leisha hopes that her TEDx Talk and her passion for numbers and sustainability will continue to set a positive example for professionals in the business world and beyond.

THE PRODUCT DESIGNER

Context:
Ecovative

Role:
CEO and Co-Founder

Achievement:
Design products that don't require a lot of scarce material and whose components can easily be composted and returned to the Earth

While Eben Bayer was still pursuing his double major in Mechanical Engineering and Innovation & Design at Rensselaer Polytechnic Institute, he started exploring how mushrooms could serve as natural glue or resin. "Nature is what inspired me to get started in sustainable design," the CEO of Ecovative says. Having grown up on a farm in Vermont, Eben had observed how tiny white fibers, mycelium, were holding wood chips together. "I'm always looking to nature for inspiration on how we can create materials with better processes," he adds.

With a degree in his pocket, Eben co-founded Ecovative in 2007. The company, which currently employs 75 people and whose clients include Dell, Gunlocke, and Steelcase, produces plastic alternatives for packaging, insulation, and building materials from local agricultural waste like corn stalks. During the process, mycelium is introduced, binding the loose particles together. "We grow these products inside a custom mold. The resulting materials are completely natural and home compostable," Eben explains. It's mushroom magic!

Of course, biological materials pose some challenges, he admits. "For instance, our materials need to be within a certain thickness range to ensure that there's enough material for the mycelium to have robust and healthy growth, but there can't be so much material that the mycelium doesn't receive oxygen in the middle or bottom of the part.

All of our equipment has been custom built to be compatible with our living organism, so whenever we have a new design idea, we simply need to make sure we have the compatible equipment to make it happen."

Ecovative's newest product, Myco Board™, an alternative to compressed particleboard, presents significant applications for the business, Eben says. "These engineered wood products are typically produced by using toxic chemicals to bind the timber particles together. We can replace the use of urea-formaldehyde in these products with our fire resistant, natural organism." Based on Cradle to Cradle principles, Ecovative's products and process have achieved a Gold level certification. To date, the company has made over one million pounds of mushroom materials that create zero waste. "We upcycle agricultural waste . . . and then it returns back to nature at the end of its useful life. Our products displace petroleum-based foams and urea-formaldehyde resins that are harmful to users and to the planet."

Nature's synergetic relationships also inform Eben Bayer's leadership style. "I value understanding and respecting people's varying talents, and harnessing that for the furthering of the employee and business. Encouraging people to try something new without the fear of failure is also important to me. I think collaboration is essential for the furthering of products and ideas. To keep the collaborative nature of the company, we host regularly scheduled events that allow us to share information across the organization and encourage feedback and input from our different departments."

To Eben, becoming a sustainable professional starts by identifying a problem that needs to be solved, not just an idea that might be profitable. "Look to nature for your solutions, either by taking inspiration from nature on how to improve a man-made process, or by actually utilizing something that happens in nature. And prepare to be not just competitive with the traditional options, but to have to outperform them."

THE ORGANIC FARMER

Context:
Organic Valley Co-op

Role:
Organic Dairy Farmer

Achievement:
Turn a conventional farm into an organic dairy and improve the health of livestock, soil, and people

In the early 1990's, Gary Mosgaller nearly lost his eyesight in a work-related accident. He was about to open a chemical herbicide when the container flashed back, and the toxic liquid sprayed into his eyes. Had he not immediately reached for a nearby water hose, he would have gone blind. That day, Mosgaller, a third-generation dairy farmer from northeastern Wisconsin – or "the thumb that sticks out," as he likes to say – had an epiphany. "This is not right!" he thought. Earlier he had also suffered from a rash as a result of being exposed to the many chemicals conventional farmers regularly have to apply to their crops. He knew something had to change, he says.

"I was looking to get out of the system," Mosgaller remembers, referring to the hamster wheel-like dependency many modern farmers get caught up in when they use genetically-modified seeds that require specific chemicals produced exclusively by large agro-chemical companies. "You buy their seeds, and you do what they want. It's prescription farming . . . That's how farming got off track. I didn't like what I was doing." Mosgaller had children and "didn't want them to be exposed to those hazards." He also objected to the way the livestock was treated in conventional operations. However, the transition to becoming an organic farmer was not easy. "It's a learning curve. At that time, there wasn't so much information. I had to learn to get back into pastures." Luckily, Mosgaller adds, one of his neighbors also decided to transition to organic farming at the same time, so they were able to support each other.

Mosgaller's 420-acre farm was home to about 60 cows. "Being a dairy, I converted all the land on which I had previously grown corn and other crops into pasture. Now the cows graze on paddocks that are fenced off. They're getting fresh feed every day, and it keeps you in contact with them. They come up and rub up on you." In conventional dairy farms, this would be unthinkable, he explains.

His neighbors first gave him a hard time and questioned he would be able to make it financially. "They all thought I would fail," he recalls. Moreover, his veterinarian told him: "You can't farm like that. You need antibiotics." Mosgaller turned to alternative remedies instead. Antibiotics can have side effects and their widespread use in livestock production has also been blamed for the increase in resistant bacteria. "I just wanted everything to be safe," Mosgaller justifies his decision.

In spite of his neighbors' dire predictions, Mosgaller could see that the new farming methods made a difference. "After I went organic, the animal health improved dramatically. The soil, the plants all got healthier." The soil's fertility initially posed another challenge for the organic farmer, but he soon discovered that "when there's a need, someone will think of a solution." In this case, it came in the form of composted chicken manure pellets that he started using. "I think that creating good food makes you feel good. As an organic farmer, you're listening more, observing everything around you," Mosgaller sums up his experience.

When asked what advice he would give young farmers about going the organic route, he contends: "I'd say go for it. Consumers are asking for it. Don't get sidetracked by the numbers . . . as far as the future goes, organic farming has a lot to offer." In his office, Mosgaller keeps a sign with a quote by Wes Jackson, the founder and president of The Land Institute: "*It's better to trust the wisdom of nature than the cleverness of man.*" – "It's so simple!" Mosgaller concludes.

THE SOCIAL WORKER

Context:
Merle Wexler, Miami, Florida

Role:
Champion

Achievement:
Stand up for the weak if they themselves cannot do that (sufficiently)

Merle is the "voice" of five children. After retiring from her position as a social worker at Big Brothers Big Sisters of Greater Miami, where she worked for 32 years matching children of single parents to like-minded volunteers, she now dedicates her time to the city's Guardian ad Litem program, representing children who are in Dependency Court. These youngsters have been removed from their parents or relatives for abuse or neglect issues, and a family court judge will frequently request a *guardian ad litem* to become the children's advocate.

"Children need to be heard," Merle explains. "They are our future, and they can only learn if given opportunities for self-expression. In return, I learn a great deal from them: the ability to laugh, to be silly, and to be affectionate. Such experiences better me, and, as a result, I can give more to others." We live in a system that often doesn't work well, Merle thinks. Her role is to do all she can to help get the necessary services for "[her] kids." Sometimes, she actually gets the system to reverse itself and look at the child as a person, not a number. When this happens, Merle feels delighted for the child and – to be honest – for herself, she confesses.

Having seen many children being denied the services and attention that they so desperately need from a system that is overloaded with crisis after crisis, Merle decided to put her professional expertise to use and to speak up on their behalf. "Judges and attorneys don't have the luxury of time to investigate the back story of what is going on in a child's life; as a Guardian ad Litem I make calls, talk to others associated with the case, and report my findings to the attorney, who will then present this information at a court hearing."

A recent case, she says, has touched her heart deeply: C. and C., two-year-old twin girls, who were removed from their birth mother's care when they were only three months old and have lived with their paternal grandmother ever since. Their mother has stated that she wants to be "reunified" with her girls, but the judge has expressed doubt. There are many reasons why such a reunification is a scary process. The twins suffer from sickle cell anemia, which, if not monitored consistently, can bring about lethal consequences. The mother, Merle explains, had been granted unsupervised visits, but those visits were disastrous because the mother did not look after her twin daughters well, and their medical needs were ignored.

According to Merle, the twins' mother is a very explosive person, oppositional and a good "talker," but her actions have not supported her words. Merle's job has been to reach out to the other therapeutic services the mother has been assigned to and get feedback that is then presented to the judge. At times, she even personally addresses the judge. "I am very concerned about keeping these girls safe, both physically and emotionally, and I feel a sense of duty to speak for them. I am impartial and want ONLY what is best for them," Merle explains.

When people ask Merle if dealing with "poor people" or "people who have problems" or who live "in poor neighborhoods" depresses her, she always counters that it's quite the opposite. Rather than become depressed, she feels enriched by human differences. Without diversity, Merle tells those who question her, life would be boring. Looking back at a life-long career, Merle is as enthusiastic about her profession as ever: "There hasn't been a day when I didn't want to go to the office," she says. "Many of the children in my care have gone on to become writers, dentists, chefs, and even presidents of banks." Their love and trust have shown Merle what strength truly means, and that's why she feels that standing up for the weak and lending them a voice is what being a social worker is all about.

THE RESEARCHER

Context:
University of Florida, Division of Infectious Diseases & Global Medicine

Role:
Assistant Professor of Medicine

Achievement:
Deliver valuable, societally relevant, and applicable scientific knowledge and insights

Ideally, science is value-free, objective and independent. Ideally, science studies reality from a certain distance, without ever being involved in it itself. Such an involvement would be unacceptable; it would corrupt the purity of the academic researcher.

This is the classical image of the academic research world, but over the course of the twentieth century, it has become clear that such a view should not be maintained. Science philosophers like Stephen Toulmin, Paul Feyerabend, and Bruno Latour have stated that value-free science is impossible. New movements such as Marxist science and feminist science, which did not even *want* to be value-free, arose from society. Moreover, for years, large research studies have been performed or sponsored by companies with vested interests. Think about the pharmaceutical, oil, weapons, and tobacco industries. Science has also been plagued by questionable practices involving scientists creating or embellishing data. Scientists, after all, appear to be ordinary people.

However, there is another side to this. Is the neutrality and objectivity of scientific research always desirable? When you conduct research into aspects of (un)sustainability, for example, to combat climate change, poverty, or disease, you cannot deny that, as a scientist, you are trying to achieve certain desired results that will contribute to a better world.

"My strong belief is that we're never neutral – we're human," Dr. Amy Yomiko Vittor says. "Furthermore, I feel the onus is on us to advocate for those we're serving." Dr. Vittor's views have been shaped by years of experience in the field. While still in middle school, she became curious about the environment and humanity's impact on it. "I was informed by the Buddhist concept of Oneness of Self and Environment instilled by my parents and mentor, Daisaku Ikeda," remembers Professor Vittor, whose mother is Japanese. Since then, Vittor has pondered questions like: "How are we shaping the environment, and how is it shaping us?" The notion that "we are one with our environment" still guides her as a person and a professional, she contends. "Our destinies are joined, and this should inform the actions we take."

Since her first research project in Costa Rica as an undergraduate student at the University of California at Berkeley, Dr. Vittor has traveled extensively to investigate the connection between ecology and vector-borne diseases such as malaria, dengue, and most recently the Madariaga virus. What impacts do ecological and social conditions have on diseases these days? The infectious disease specialist believes that "the slum condition presents a social injustice that makes a vulnerable population even more vulnerable." Drinking water access, Dr. Vittor explains, can serve as an example. Unlike residents in industrialized countries, people in the developing world experience water insecurity. "We have a reliable source of water and don't have to store water in big containers and cisterns where mosquitoes breed." Unfortunately, many people around the globe do not enjoy this luxury.

In addition to dismal social conditions, climate change is thought to affect the spread of vector-borne illnesses. "We can say that mosquito vectors may be able to expand their ranges," says Dr. Vittor. For instance, she adds, Gainesville, where the University of Florida is located, currently does not have *Aedes aegypti*, the mosquito associated with the Zika virus. That may change though.

As an involved scientist, Vittor understands that successful research depends on collaboration. On an *interdisciplinary* level, she regularly interacts with other experts: geographers, statisticians, entomologists, virologists, and engineers, to name a few. "Dealing with different disciplines is a little like learning foreign languages. You have to gain enough fluency to find common ground. It's also very cross-pollinating," she says. In addition, her work involves *transdisciplinary* aspects, for instance, when she communicates with government entities like the Ministry of Health in Peru, residents in affected areas, and patients. "Just this morning, we gave a congressional briefing to folks in D.C. regarding the Zika virus," Vittor offers as an example. In short, reaching out on inter- and transdisciplinary levels is vital for sustainably competent researchers.

With regards to promoting global peace and sustainable development, Vittor hopes to inspire her students and medical residents to care deeply about their patients and the communities they research and serve. In conversations with her colleagues and students, she likes to ask: "Why do we do what we do? What's the point if we're not making the lives of those around us better? Yes, we need to publish and get grants, but we also need to think about the bigger picture." Motivated by the interconnectedness of all life, she advises: "Through our own inner transformation, each of us has the capacity to create and sustain great positive change."

It looks as though one of Amy Vittor's own projects has finally come full circle. Fifteen years ago, she says, she spent three years in the Peruvian Amazon researching the interaction between deforestation and malaria, never knowing whether the results would ever amount to anything. Now her dedication and advocacy are about to pay off. Just the day before, Dr. Vittor says, she had "a very positive conversation with a philanthropic foundation. They are thinking about using this region as a demonstration of what can be done." Let the transformation begin.

THE TEACHER

Context:
Air Base K-8 Center, Homestead, Florida

Role:
Elementary school teacher

Achievement:
Raise love for nature and find a didactic approach fitting for each individual child, instill a sense of wonderment, and help students to discover and value their world while simultaneously empowering them to act sustainably

"I had to take a cold, 5-minute shower last night!" the mother of one of Hannah Purcell's 6th grade students complained when picking up her daughter. The class had been discussing energy and water conservation methods, and many students carried that message back home, some confronting their parents directly. Since Hannah Purcell started teaching at Air Base K-8 Center, an international magnet school in Homestead, Florida, eight years ago, she has made the environment an essential part of her curriculum, spearheading a number of green initiatives that have won the school awards and even got her students invited to present at a sustainability exposition at Florida International University.

Growing up on military bases in different European countries, Purcell experienced "a lifestyle of appreciation of nature." She felt a "huge gap" when her family returned to the United States. Suddenly everything was materialistic and there was little to no nature, she recalled. Later, as an elementary school teacher, she saw the school as "a blank canvas with lots of empty lawn." Purcell imagined a more engaging schoolyard and created a small garden. Administrators said she was wasting her time. However, soon even the "tough" students took an interest. "What are you doing, Miss?" they asked, volunteering to help plant or pull weeds.

At her current school, the gardens are now school wide. On Beautification Days families, teachers, and volunteers build gardens, decorate walls with environmental messages, and create signage about seed germination and native species. Walking down "Milkweed Way," one sees a shade house, a butterfly garden, an outdoor classroom, a wildflower meadow, a display of garden certifications, rain barrels, bird baths, compost and recycling bins, and a row of poles adorned with colorful painted butterflies – Purcell calls this their "learning gardens."

In spite of obstacles, Purcell spearheaded programs and projects, securing grants from local businesses, organizing fundraisers, obtaining resources, and getting other teachers on board. "I'm a very persistent person. You're changing a mindset, a culture, which takes time," she said smiling. A few years ago, she proposed Deering Estate's N.E.S.T.T. (Nurturing Environmental Stewards of Today and

Tomorrow), helping it expand from a pilot of 15 students to three grade levels. Another example is the Green Education Fair, where she invites green agencies to share their expertise with everyone. She also formed the Environmental Ambassadors Club, whose members present environmental problems and solutions to other students and the community. Ms. Purcell speaks proudly of her "school family" and the amazing leadership of Principal Raul Calzadilla, Jr. – "They are the reason for our success."

Located near a military base in a mostly rural area, the school serves culturally and ethnically diverse students, including those from military families. When Purcell's students learned about pesticides and their effect on endangered butterflies and human health, they quickly recognized the problem. "Kids see systems and when empowered, they want to take action," Purcell explained. Several years ago, they presented to the local mayor and city council on the importance and benefits of native plants, organic farming, and recycling. The environmental chief of Homestead Air Reserve Base was impressed and invited Purcell's students to annually tour the base to learn how it uses solar energy, reclaims water, reduces waste, and recycles. Everyone was fascinated. Hannah Purcell believes that her students "get it" because she hears the proof in their conversations and sees it in their actions. She is hopeful they will continue being stewards of the environment and having a positive impact on sustainability issues.

At the end of the school tour, a group of girls, concerned expressions on their faces, ran up to us. "Please, Ms. Purcell, you've got to come. There's an injured bird!" – "Yep, that's part of my job," this inspiring educator explained, wishing me a good afternoon before being pulled away by several little hands.

CHAPTER TWELVE
Action skills

The Competence (Figure 12.1):

A sustainably competent professional is decisive and capable of acting.

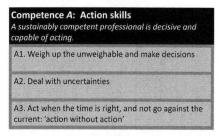
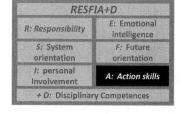

Figure 12.1 *Competence A: Action skills*

Responsibility, emotional intelligence, ethical awareness, passion, and idealism – these are all important characteristics of a sustainably competent professional, and they were all discussed in previous chapters. However, there is one other characteristic without which all these competences are not worth much: the ability to cut the Gordian knot and spring into action. This is the final competence of this book, and you will find it in the present chapter.

Below are the three achievements I will tell you about in this chapter:

- *Weigh up the unweighable and make decisions*
- *Deal with uncertainties*
- *Act when the time is right, and do not go against the current: "action without action"*

For one of my earlier books, I created a series of tasks for my students. One of them involved a letter – not a real one. Gagnon Foods does not exist – I made it up – and both Mr. Rodriguez and Mr. Howard are fictitious, too. As I will show you, the letter illustrates the topics of this chapter. Please read the letter first.

To Mr. Rodriguez,
Manager of Gagnon Foods

Dear Mr. Rodriguez,

I am employed in your Packaging Department, but maybe not for much longer as I fear you will soon fire me. This is because I believe your plans will never work for this company. Mr. Rodriguez, I am well aware that five years ago, you promised that within five years (i.e. now), you would have gotten rid of child labor in our factory in Rajasthan (India). Those children who have to work so hard for you are facing a terrible fate.

Five years ago, the company was doing great, so it was easy to promise something like this, but last year, things started going belly-up and you had to dismiss 20 of my coworkers. I'm pretty sure we were already on the brink of bankruptcy then. Five years ago, you also promised that we would stop buying rice in Rajasthan within five years' time since they were using poison to get rid of insects, which is bad to the environment. Just last month, you explained in the Gagnon newsletter "Rice and Beans" that it might cost the company money, but that we had to do it because it was socially responsible, and we had to focus on corporate social responsibility. But now I want to ask you: how responsible was this move when you have to fire so many people – people like me? Surely you cannot do that?

I understand that the children in Rajasthan are very young to be working for Gagnon, especially if – as you say – they are only eight years old. But if you fire them and instead hire a group of adults, the latter will certainly be more expensive! Can you cover those additional costs? I don't think so!

Mr. Rodriguez, I am now 50 years old, and I have worked for your company for 32 years. I worked hard I must add. If I am fired now,

I'll never find another job. I could hit rock bottom and may even start drinking. My wife spends the whole day crying because she is so afraid. She says we should phone somebody at the newspaper or television news. I think that may be a good idea.

Please, Mr. Rodriguez, don't fire those kids in India. And the rice with the stuff to kill bugs, we've been selling it for at least 50 years, so why would our customers want to change? There's no reason to suddenly stop selling it. Please save me because I'll be out of options if I were to lose my job!

Your faithful employee,

John Howard

There are a lot of aspects to this letter. You can apply the *Triple P* nicely: the people aspects are, for example, child labor in Rajasthan and the fears of John Howard and his wife. The planet aspect is apparent in "the stuff to kill bugs" that damages the environment and in the growth of rice, of course. There are also plenty of profit aspects, varying from the higher salary burden when children are replaced by adults to a recent near bankruptcy and the dismissal of 20 employees. When everything was going well, Manager Rodriguez once made a promise that he now feels bound to, but can he live up to it? He faces a nasty dilemma: he will have to weigh issues against each other that are totally incomparable – unweighable. Which is more important: abolishing child labor, saving the environment, or guaranteeing the employees' jobs? How do you weigh these against each other, for heaven's sake?

Weigh up the unweighable is one of the achievements this chapter is about. Another achievement is *dealing with uncertainties*, and Mr. Howard's letter contains a number of them. There is uncertainty for manager Rodriguez: will the company survive when child labor is banned? Will the harvest be bountiful enough if the rice is grown without pesticides, and how stable will it be in the following years? Will the customers buy the rice, or rather, will they perhaps even demand it? There is uncertainty, too, for Mr. Howard, and probably for many of his colleagues. Will he keep his job? Will he end up in the gutter?

The third achievement in this chapter deals with *acting when the time is right*. Did Mr. Rodriguez do that five years ago when he made his socially responsible promises? And right now, how can he deal with the present crisis effectively? He must decide how to save the company and keep his personnel satisfied. Also, to what extent can he live up to the promises that are inspired by his conscience?

In the task that involves the letter, students have to discuss the situation and make decisions. I have done the exercise a few times with groups of employees, and I can assure you that it created quite a stir. I won't bother you with that now. Instead, I will offer you the stories of professionals who dealt with tough situations in a decisive way.

12.1 WEIGH UP THE UNWEIGHABLE

"Negotiating with people that have blood on their hands presents a dilemma for a peace movement. It is a predicament about choices that you can't weigh against each other. Which is more important: justice or peace?"

This was the dilemma of Jan Gruiters, director of the peace organization PAX. Without a doubt, Joseph Kony, the leader of the infamous Lord's Resistance Army (LRA), consisting mainly of kidnapped child soldiers, had blood on his hands. He founded the rebel group in 1987 with the intention off seizing power in Uganda.

For decades, Joseph Kony, one of the most atrocious warlords in Africa, has in one way or another been able to escape from attempts to capture or kill him. The people living in the countries where the LRA practices its terror – Uganda, Sudan, and Congo – were desperate. What should they do? Negotiate? About what? A safe haven for war criminal Kony, indicted by the International Criminal Court (ICC), in exchange for peace? This would mean that Kony would elude justice! Hence, Jan Gruiters' concern: what should weigh more, justice or peace?

"After graduating with a degree in information technology, I switched from a potentially successful career in the world of automation to an uncertain existence within the peace movement," Jan Gruiters writes. "In the peace movement, I was able to dedicate my time to what I really found meaningful: war and peace. That personal decision was partly based on World War II, the moral benchmark for the post-war generation.

Driven by ideals, I threw myself into the peace movement. Who was good, who was bad? In those days, it seemed evident. Nelson Mandela was good; the apartheid regime in South Africa was bad. Vaclav Havel was good; the communist government in (the former) Czechoslovakia was bad. Bishop Oscar Romero was good; the military dictatorship in El Salvador was bad.

Through the years, my ideals have not worn out, but for the contemporary wars, the boundaries between good and bad, right and wrong, victims and culprits often seem much less clear. The boundary between perpetration and victimization frequently runs through the heart of one person. To what degree is a child soldier who unscrupulously rapes women an offender or a victim? Is he to be held accountable for his crimes or excused because of a lack of sound societal conditions? Should he be tried or helped?

It becomes even harder when, in order for peace negotiations to begin, it is inevitable to negotiate with people who have blood on their hands, with war criminals who should be in a criminal court rather than at the negotiation table. These are not questions but real dilemmas that belong to the work of a peace organization."

In his fascinating book *No More War – Winning Mission or Lost Vision*, which was published in Dutch in 2012, Gruiters writes on a scientific level about dilemmas concerning war and peace. However, Gruiters is not just a theorist. In his work as a director for PAX, he and his organization were repeatedly forced to make painful moral decisions.

"The negotiations with the Lord's Resistance Army, led by the sinister Joseph Kony, against whom an arrest warrant was issued by the International Criminal Court in The Hague, were a striking example. The violence and raids by the LRA have forced millions of people to flee, mainly Uganda and South Sudan. The LRA kidnapped thousands of children, killed thousands of people. No one succeeded in defeating the LRA or in arresting its leadership. PAX mediated between Joseph Kony and the governments of Uganda and South Sudan, which brought, at least for some time, a truce enabling refugees to return home."

It was a tough decision, and not everyone agreed with Gruiters. In his letter to me, Gruiters explains how he arrived at his decision.

"Regarding its peace work, PAX is guided by human dignity as its core value. Every human being has a right to a dignified life. Human dignity is the ultimate yardstick for our peace work, based on how we account for our activities to ourselves and to society. Local communities in Uganda and South Sudan invited us to mediate the conflict with the LRA. They were yearning for a dignified existence. The violence, which had created so many victims and would cause many more if nothing was done, had to be stopped. Mediating the conflict was more urgent than simply bringing Joseph Kony to court. The human dignity of innocent civilians weighed the heaviest, not our sense of justice. It was a choice that raised a lot of discussion within and outside of the peace movement."

PAX first attempted to start negotiations in 1998, but neither Kony nor the governments of Uganda and Sudan were prepared to negotiate. Only toward the end of 2005 did PAX formally receive the request from Sudan and the LRA to mediate between the parties. It was not until May 18, 2006, that newspapers reported President Museveni of Uganda was also prepared to join. For a number of years, violence decreased, but regrettably it did not last. In 2012, the international attention for the drama of the LRA increased strongly and attempts to catch Kony intensified. This was partly due to an impressive documentary called "Kony 2012," which was placed on YouTube by the organization Invisible Children, Inc. and viewed a hundred million times within a month. Even though negotiations did not lead to a peace treaty, violence has since declined. But at the time I am writing this text, Kony and his LRA are still wandering freely. The international community does not seem prepared to launch serious attempts to arrest him.

"The reality of armed conflicts confronts us with complex dilemmas," Gruiters writes, "dilemmas that go beyond the simple schemes of good and bad. In situations where we have to weigh the unweighable rationally and emotionally, we are well advised to make the values that are guiding the actions of humans explicit. In such cases, we have to rely on our moral yardstick. It is not the functional rationality that is so dominantly available in our times but the orientation toward values that can help us weigh the dilemmas properly and make decisions. It implies that a choice to be made in a stubborn reality of war or peace is often a choice for the lesser evil."

THE ACHIEVEMENT

You weigh up the unweighable and make decisions.

This means:

- *You recognize and acknowledge situations in your professional activities in which interests that cannot be compared in an unambiguous way have to be weighed against each other.*
- *You discuss decisions with the involved stakeholders or their representatives. You consider the values of all those who have an interest in these decisions, including yourself.*
- *Partially based on this, you rationally weigh the pros and cons and make decisions. You explain your decisions to the stakeholders or their representatives.*
- *You investigate whether there are options to make the conflicting interests less so. You investigate whether there are ways to compensate those who suffer from the negative consequences of your decisions.*

Incompatible interests are not only found in the area of war and peace but also in the following examples: starting a company that is beneficial for the local economy but detrimental for the local environment; offering extra care for students or patients at the expense of less care for other students or patients or your own health or well-being; designing a product that causes fewer emissions of greenhouse gases but demands more scarce materials; setting up activities for underprivileged young people in a way that makes nearby residents unhappy – "nimby" (not in my backyard)!

Sometimes such dilemmas are about conflicting interests of people versus planet, for instance, when you grow crops for biofuel: good against climate change but bad for poor people since the increasing demand for agricultural land leads to higher food prices.

Sometimes it is about the interests of profit versus people, for instance, when you combat child labor or try to raise extremely low wages while harming the competitive position of certain companies.

It may even be about people versus people. When you revitalize urban neighborhoods, residents welcome the change until they can no longer afford the rent. In this case, wealthier people moving into the newly gentrified areas benefit.

In short, when it comes to complex sustainability issues, there are hardly any simple, straightforward solutions. That's how life is. A sustainably competent professional does not have to find all this easy, but he or she will eventually find ways to deal with these challenges.

Stakeholders are not always able to defend their interests themselves. In that case, representatives can do it for them. If children are concerned, you may think of parent organizations or of Child Protective Services. Mentally challenged people have their own organizations, too. When animals, or more generally speaking, nature or the environment are stakeholders, all kinds of action groups exist, varying from local groups such as "Friends of the Crooked River" in Ohio to national organizations like the Sierra Club to global ones like the World Wildlife Fund (WWF).

It is possible to compensate for harmful consequences, for example, by planting trees as a CO_2 offset or by paying compensation for lost nature. If understaffing causes problems, you can expand your team to offer sufficient care for all students or patients. If noise pollution bothers nearby residents, build a sound barrier and make sure you select biodegradable materials.

12.2 DEAL WITH UNCERTAINTIES

Action skills, the topic of this chapter, may not only be hindered by nearly impossible dilemmas but also by a lack of certainties. The future is unknown. What will happen in the coming months, years, or decades? Nobody knows. But also the present – and even the past – are not fully known. If you get paralyzed by uncertainty or fear as a professional, your ability to make decisions and your action skills go down the drain.

One way to deal with uncertainties is the use of a technique called "backcasting." Why is this process called "backcasting?" Most notably, forecasting is impossible due to the many uncertainties. As lots of trend watchers and futurologists keep proving to us over and over: the future is unpredictable! With backcasting, you don't go from the present to the future, but quite the opposite, you move backward from a range of possible futures toward now. This enables a group of creative people to explore all kinds of futures and decide which of them are appealing and which are not. They can then determine which steps to take *now* to make the appealing scenarios more likely, and also which steps will most certainly *not* lead there.

Someone who applies this tool regularly as part of his job is Pong Leung, Senior Associate for The Natural Step, Canada, a non-profit organization that offers sustainability consulting involving backcasting to individuals, businesses, municipalities, and institutions. While still in college, Pong read Paul Hawken's *The Ecology of Commerce* and found it inspiring. "In business school, they didn't talk about sustainability," he says, but the topic fascinated him, and he had "a lot of questions about it." Eventually, he obtained a Master's of Science in environmental management and policy at the International Institute for Industrial Environmental Economics at Lund University in Sweden and joined The Natural Step.

One of Pong's recent clients, ISL Engineering and Land Services, approached him after a survey of their 50 largest clients had revealed sustainability as their most important need and the fact that ISL's employees had started their own green team. At the initial meeting with ISL's leadership, Pong and his colleagues guided the conversation in a strategic direction: "The first thing we try to do is find out what the strategic relevance of sustainability is for them. For example, we often share three areas where we have found sustainability to create lasting value: enhancing brand reputation, driving innovation, and fostering a culture of excellence. One or more of them will resonate, and then we explore that further. It is important that we explore the "why", because backcasting is an investment."

To help understand the "why", they first help the business take stock of the current situation via stakeholder interviews, surveys, a review of key documents, and a best practices scan. "Change is uncomfortable. It's disruptive," Pong admits, "but companies see the writing on the wall . . . In interview sessions with the senior leaders, we get a sense of the company's hopes and fears." A lot of times, he says, demands from stakeholders convince companies to embrace sustainability. "You can ignore your stakeholders, but is that smart?" Pong asks.

This sets the stage to apply backcasting via the *ABCD* method pioneered by The Natural Step. Pong leads his clients from *Awareness* and Visioning to *Baseline* Mapping, i.e. a "gap analysis", and from there to *Creative* Solutions and *Deciding* on Priorities. "We help the organization integrate sustainability into their strategy, culture and operations. They recognize that it means starting with the end in mind, and taking an honest look at their current situation . . . As a company, you want to build on your strengths, but you are also looking to move to a different place."

Clarifying the gap between desired future and current reality allows groups to make decisions on actions in spite of uncertainties by answering three key questions: "Does it move us in the right direction? Is it a flexible platform for future steps? And does it generate sufficient return on investment? In short, does it make business sense in the near- and long-term? We try to make the sessions interactive and help them align with the future they want to create," Pong explains.

The consulting typically takes place over an extended time. Pong says, "We always frame it as a 3–7 year change initiative. During the first three years, we are more actively involved. Then less as sustainability becomes part of the company's culture. When there are bumps in the road or when specific issues arise, we come in for a boost." In ISL's case, the efforts paid off. Not long after the initial engagement, it was included on the Green 30 list as one of Canada's most environmentally progressive employers.

What Pong Leung enjoys most about his job is "helping others make a difference and helping organizations move forward." Especially now that he has children, he feels that "work isn't just what you do for a living; it's making a contribution." In the end, the consultant's job is finished not after handing over pieces of advice but when clients have the capacity to arrive at their own conclusions in the face of uncertainty.

THE ACHIEVEMENT

You deal with uncertainties.

This means:

- *You carefully estimate the level of uncertainty of the information you use for your professional activities.*
- *You plan your professional activities while taking uncertainties into consideration; if necessary, you take appropriate actions.*

- *You apply the precautionary principle: You choose your plans and methods in a way that minimizes uncertainties of crucial importance whenever possible.*
- *You apply effective methods to reach responsible and accepted decisions, taking into account the inevitable uncertainties.*

Uncertainty can result from a variety of causes. You may think of:

- *uncertainty due to a lack of information, inaccurate information, potentially unreliable information, or information from contradicting sources.*
- *uncertainty about delivery times, purchase prices, markets, legal regulations, or your own production quality.*
- *uncertainty about applied scientific models or technological or medical solutions. Have they been proved accurate ("evidence based")? Are they sufficiently accepted?*
- *uncertainty about the reactions you may get to certain events or developments, for instance, to decisions you might make. This may involve reactions to physical systems (a machine, a plant, a forest, a robot), but it may also involve a person or a group of people (customers, clients, student, or patients; the staff, the union, a country).*
- *uncertainty about support or resistance you may receive.*
- *uncertainty regarding the whims of the system. What is true today may turn out to be a lie tomorrow.*
- *uncertainty about shifting values: what is important, and who gets to decide?*
- *finally, uncertainty about yourself: do I want this? Can I do it? Do I have the guts? Do I possess the necessary perseverance?*

You can deal with uncertainties in many ways. You may postpone decisions and first seek more information, for instance, by conducting additional research to support a claim, perhaps preceded by a stakeholder analysis. Of course, you can also sit back and make no decision at all. You probably know that this does not work well: no decision is a decision, too. If you do nothing and freeze, the world does not freeze, and eventually everything will overwhelm you. Nevertheless, sometimes the "zero option" may be a good decision since certain problems that you were initially very worried about all of a sudden stop being problems, disappearing like snow under the heat of the sun. Have you seen it happen?

You may also deal with uncertainties by minimizing the risks of potentially negative effects. In that case, you apply the *precautionary principle*.

Do you have insurance? Probably you do. Most likely, you have a bunch of different policies: against fire, burglary, disease, accidents, car trouble, liability, unemployment, death, etc. In addition, you have probably taken other precautions such as locks on the door, a bicycle pump, spare keys, condoms, bandages, vaccinations, and an emergency fund. Collectively, we even have much more: the fire brigade, the police, the Armed Forces, levees, early warning systems, disaster plans, emergency supplies, and a vice-president. They are all expressions of the precautionary principle. In short, everybody safeguards against something that *might* go wrong.

To sustainability, the precautionary principle is highly relevant. As metals, oil, and gas will (likely) become more expensive in the future because of scarcity and depletion, many companies are investing in alternative materials and sustainable sources of energy. The debates about climate change are still continuing (and may do so indefinitely), and yet, governments and companies spend billions to combat the negative effects.

Unweighable considerations weighed.

Impossible decisions made.

Confounding uncertainties overcome or passed.

Time for action.

12.3 ACTION WITHOUT ACTION

Doing without doing; action without action – a nice paradox. It sounds impossible, but it isn't since the first "action" means something different than the second. The first "action" stands for "achieve something, act successfully." The second "action" signifies "force, push, impose, and exert pressure." In other words, "action without action" implies: "be effective without forcing, or act at the right moment, in a suitable way."

The expression "action without action," which comes from Chinese – where it sounds like *wei wu wei* – has existed for a long time. The principle stems from the Tao Te Ching (or Daoteching), the famous book by the Chinese philosopher Lao Tzu (or Laozi), the founder of Taoism (Daoism), who lived probably between 600–500 BCE. The principle is easy to understand. Imagine a child sitting on a swing, asking you to push. Of course, you give the first push only once the child is sitting down and holding on firmly. But the second and successive ones? You'd better not push at the moment when the child comes flying toward you at full speed. If you do, you will definitely break the momentum and perhaps even your wrist. The best you can do is wait until the swing roughly reaches its highest point of motion, and then give a light push. This does not require much strength. A series of such pushes, given at just the right moment, adds up to a fabulous result. That is "action without action." Swimming in a river, along with the current as opposed to against it or across, also captures the principle of action without action – making use of existing forces and motions instead of fighting them.

Having studied under recognized Master Meng Zhiling, Vice-President of the Chinese Taoist Association, David Hessler believes that "*wu wei* should be applied to everywhere in one's life." Hessler, the founder of the US Taoist Association, leads student trips to China and teaches history at Montclair Kimberley Academy in New Jersey. He shares a story Master Meng told him:

One day, Master Meng, who was living as a hermit in the mountains, was approached by local villagers with a question. The villagers had invested in a power company, but recently, the machines weren't working properly, and now they were losing money. Apparently, previously, there had been an older man in charge, but the villagers felt he never did anything, so they had fired him and instead had hired two younger men who understood technology well. However, things hadn't gotten better, the villagers lamented. What should they do, they asked? Master Meng listened carefully and finally advised, "Hire the old mechanic back." The villagers were perplexed. "But he never did anything," they said. "Exactly!" Master Meng explained. The old mechanic did not have to do anything because he understood when to act, solving minor issues before they became big problems, thus making it seem effortless – action at the right moment. If the older man trained the younger men to practice *wu wei*, they, too, would learn to recognize potential trouble in time, the hermit told them.

"Acting at the 'right moment' is acting according to *wu wei*," Hessler argues. "But it is also understanding the nature of the situation one is in and what is required of the person at that moment. The way one understands what is the right moment is complicated. That comes when one can see the situation clearly without personal prejudice or bias. When you can do that, then you see any situation very clearly and act in accordance with what is actually called for."

To help his own high school students better understand *wu wei*, Hessler engages them with examples from sports, for example, soccer or basketball. An experienced point guard, he tells them, knows precisely when a teammate will be in an open space and passes the ball at just the right moment without having to think about it. When players are in the "zone" or in the "flow," dribbling and shooting become second nature just like walking or breathing. "You're acting without an ego," Hessler says. "Maybe the best metaphor for *wu wei* is water: It never forces things but goes under or around when its way is blocked. Also, water benefits without seeking attention. All life depends on water."

As an educator, Hessler applies *wu wei* in his daily work and recently published an article called "Teaching with Tao" in the *Journal of Daoist Studies*. "If the teacher understands the nature of the student, for example, whether he or she is a visual or an auditory learner, then the teacher automatically adjusts. An experienced teacher doesn't have to think about it. He or she just does it. It's not about you, but about the student. Master Meng always cautions his followers not to seek attention and fame."

So, how can you learn to act without acting – or at just the right moment? The answer begins with creating that open space in your mind. "All of this is predicated on the fact that you have to have a mind that is quiet so that you can see clearly what the next thing that needs to be done is," Hessler, who has been meditating for over ten years, suggests. *Wu wei*, Hessler thinks, ultimately "has to do with what the best benefit is. It's about *you* going through life in the most ethical way. That's a hard thing to do. It's not like you adopt it. You begin to think about it, and then – gradually – it begins to become a part of you."

THE ACHIEVEMENT

You act when the time is right, and do not go against the current: "action without action."

This means:

- *You act at the right moment. No sooner, no later.*
- *You endeavor to acquire the largest possible support, if possible even consensus.*
- *For this purpose, you estimate the resistance stakeholders might have against the intended actions. You discover at which moment this resistance may be relatively low, and you design the time schedule accordingly.*
- *If you discover that resistance will diminish too slowly or not at all, or in order to increase support, you redesign your activities, aiming at a more acceptable process and result. You involve the stakeholders in this process.*

An important reason to wait for the right moment to do something is when you encounter resistance. It can be present within individuals or even in groups. However, the timing of physical systems may also cause resistance, for example, industrial processes, delivery times, biological systems, train failures, traffic jams, the unpredictable weather, or the season.

Sometimes resistance is hidden within "pretexts." As a consultant, I have heard repeatedly from certain managers that it was not a good time to introduce sustainability or CSR at the moment: "as the organization is in the middle of a change process right now."

When determining exactly at which moment the resistance of individuals or groups is minimal, you should, of course, refrain from taking advantage of the circumstances, for instance, when the involved persons are absent (due to a holiday) or vulnerable (due to illness, fatigue, or distracted attention). What you can do is wait until the support from the involved parties has grown. You might also wait until they are in a suitable state to consider the actions. You could also actively stimulate the decision process, for instance, by providing information, resolving misunderstandings, and listening actively to objections. Search for alternatives together. Set up preparatory activities ("plow the land and sow before you start harvesting") in such a way that resistance doesn't increase but diminishes. Start or restart discussions that involve all stakeholders in an equal way.

CHAPTER THIRTEEN
All the competences of the rainbow

That's it! The set of sustainability competences is complete. Chapter 11 presents a series of examples of specific competences for certain disciplines and professions. In the even-numbered chapters, 2 to 12, you can find all general competences.

All competences?

That is quite a claim, one I can never fulfill. Surely there will be people – you may be one of them – who, immediately after I make such an ambitious claim, will prove my mistake by mentioning a competence missing from my set. How about ethical consciousness, inspiration, leadership, or – if you are Christian – stewardship? In other words, how complete is this book anyway?

You see, competences are like colors; there exist an infinite number of them. If I mentioned a long series of colors and then claimed I had listed *all* of them, it would not be very hard to point out shades I had missed. There would be every chance that I didn't include Bulgarian rose, Vegas gold, or Harvard crimson, eggplant, mint, or vanilla. Perhaps I failed to mention a nameless color that is indicated by its RGB values (red-green-blue), each expressed as a number between 0 and 65,535: this offers a variation of more than 280 million shades. That's a lot, but it is *nothing* compared to the infinity of all colors. No, an enumeration of colors can never be complete.

The same applies to competences for sustainability. Whoever wants to will be able to express hundreds of them in the English language, and if you think that is still not enough, you can make up your own new words or borrow them from other languages. In short, the quest for completion is at best a hopeless effort and at worst a desperate exercise.

To deal with the enormous variety of colors, people have chosen to give names to a limited number of main colors and to consider the rest as mixtures, blends, or combinations of them. Since this has been done independently throughout many eras and in different cultures, it has rendered a fascinating diversity. Western culture traditionally distinguishes seven colors of the rainbow, plus black and white. In total, this makes a set of nine:

- *Red, orange, yellow, green, blue, indigo, violet, black, white*

However, the Candoshi, a Peruvian tribe, distinguish only eight basic colors:

- *Chobiapi, ptsiyaro, kamachpa, kavabana, tarika, kantsirpi, ponzani, borshi*

It is not easy to translate them into English, but if you try, you get something like: *red, yellow, bright green, greenish blue, purple, black, pale & grey, white.*

The Kwerba, a tribe in Irian Jaya, Indonesia, know even fewer, namely four colors:

- *Asiram, nokonum, kainanesesenum, icem*

In English, this is roughly equal to *red, yellow, green & blue & black, white.*

You're probably thinking: that's rather primitive, only four colors? Well, my hypermodern laser printer does not possess many more, as it is a five-color printer:

- *Magenta, yellow, cyan, black, white*

For four of those colors, my printer has separate toner cassettes. The fifth color, white, is produced cleverly by not using each of those four toners simultaneously. How could the Kwerba be primitive? They are hardly second to a printer from the twenty-first century!

Why are there such huge differences between color schemes? Because every scheme you design will always be a simplification of reality. What you do is cut a continuous color spectrum into a finite set of separate colors. Actually, this is simply wrong, but what are you going to do? If you don't wish to make this mistake, you can never define a color, and so we cut the rainbow into pieces: nine in Europe and North America (if you include black and white), eight with the Candoshi, four with the Kwerba, and all kinds of numbers with hundreds of different cultures.

This dividing of a continuous spectrum into a finite set of separate elements is something we do all the time, in every area. Do you want some examples from management science?

9 is the number of criteria of the EFQM Excellence Model for quality management:

  • *leadership, strategy, people, . . .*

8 is the number of fields in *Leary's Rose*:

  • *leading, helping, co-operative, . . .*

7 habits are what highly effective people possess, according to Stephen Covey:

  • *proactive, begin with the end in mind, first things first, . . .*

6 M's are basic to the *Six Sigma* method for quality management:

  • *machines, methods, materials, . . .*

5 layers together form the hierarchy of Maslow, a model for the needs and motivations of people:

  • *physiological needs, safety, social needs, . . .*

4 steps are what Deming's control cycle consists of:

  • *plan, do, check, act*

3 is the number of elements in the *Triple P* of sustainable development:

  • *people, planet, profit*

2 basic principles exist according to traditional Chinese philosophy:

  • *yang, yin*

1 is the number of universes we live in:

  • *reality*

Do you really think there are cosmic laws prescribing that a quality cycle consists of precisely four steps as Deming proposed? Of course not, and no doubt Deming realized that too. Or do you believe, as Covey taught us, that effective leaders possess exactly seven habits? Covey himself does not think so since he "discovered" an eighth habit a few years later:

- *find your voice, in other words: inspire others*

What all of these designers of the above models and systems have done is split reality into parts. While doing this, they corrupt reality, but that is *all right* as it provides us with methods to deal with reality effectively.

Mathematicians speak of a "cover." The nine criteria of the EFQM model "cover" the wide area of quality management, roughly equal to the way in which a window screen covers an open window: hermetically closed for mosquitoes and other bugs and thus effective, but not 100% closed, therefore allowing fresh air to enter.

In the same way, the sustainability competences of this book cover the wide range of competences of a sustainable professional. My spectrum (see Figure 13.1) includes:

- *responsibility, emotional intelligence, systems orientation. . .*

This is not airtight, but it is effective. If you mention competences that are not literally there, they probably present variations or combinations of competences discussed in the book. Let me illustrate this with the cases I have already cited.

Are you looking for *ethical awareness*? Go to the section on *Conscience* in Chapter 10. Do you want to find the concept of *inspiration*? Have a look at *Passion, dreams and ideals*, also in Chapter 10. Aside from that, turn to *Innovative, creative, out of the box* in Chapter 8. You are interested in *stewardship*? Search for *Responsibility* in Chapter 2, and you will find related information.

All competences?

		Stakeholder analysis
	Responsibility	Responsibility
		Transparency
		Values
	Emotional intelligence	Facts, opinions
		Interdisciplinary
		Zoom in & out (place)
	System orientation	Faults & vigors
		Integral, circular
		Zoom in & out (time)
	Future orientation	Non-linear
		Out-of-the-box
		Sustainable attitude
	personal Involvement	Passion, ideals
		Conscience
		Unweighables
	Action Skills	Uncertainties
		Action without action
+ Hundred Thousand Disciplinary Competences		

Figure 13.1 *A spectrum of a hundred thousand and eighteen competences*

Concerning *leadership*, I consider this concept to be of a different nature, not so much a competence but rather a competence *level*, so you can find it in Chapter 7, where varying degrees of leadership are explained, ranging from Apprentice (developing) to Master (advanced).

All in all this means, in my opinion, that the "rainbow" of sustainability competences in this book is complete, not in the sense of "airtight," but certainly in the sense of a "cover." Nevertheless, it could be possible that some essential competences for sustainability are truly missing from my framework. Personally, I don't expect this to be the case, but one cannot be sure. So, who knows – maybe some interesting discussions lie ahead!

CHAPTER FOURTEEN

Application of
RESFIA+D in real life

14.1 SPECIFYING THE LEVELS

In Chapter 7, I told you about levels of competence. Let me repeat them briefly:

Level 1:   Apprentice

Level 2:   Work under supervision

Level 3:   Self-direct

Level 4:   Integrate

Level 5:   Improve

Level 6:   Innovate

Level 7:   Master

As I said before (in the introduction), RESFIA+D can be used in three ways, and I am going to tell you about them in the present chapter. For all three of them, the tool is used as an assessment instrument, paving the way to create development plans: for individual professionals (14.2), for entire teams of an organization or department (14.3), or for higher education (14.4).

And finally, in 14.5: for you, in the shape of a self-test.

In order to create a genuine and practical assessment tool, it is not sufficient to define a set of levels in general terms. It will also be necessary to define those levels in some detail: specified for all different competences. This is what I did between 2007 and 2010, when I first developed and validated RESFIA+D.

For this purpose, I formulated concrete behaviors for each of the six generic competences. More precisely, I did this for all three achievements of those six competences. This resulted in separate descriptions linked to the various competence levels of all 18 (6 x 3) achievements.

Let me give you one example. For this purpose, I choose competence S: *Systems orientation*, which was discussed in Chapter 6. Out of the three achievements that were defined for this competence, I will show you S2, about *weaving faults and sources of vigor*. Chapter 6 (Section 6.2) explained:

The achievement:

You recognize flaws in the fabric and sources of vigor in systems, and you use the sources of vigor.

This means:

- *You are aware, or you investigate, which flaws in the fabric are deeply integrated in the systems with which or for which you work. These flaws are the ultimate causes of un-sustainability.*
- *You discover which sources of vigor are available in or around these systems in order to correct the flaws in the fabric. These sources of vigor are the powers we possess toward true sustainability.*
- *You succeed in effectively utilizing or mobilizing the sources of vigor, enabling you to contribute to diminish or even eradicate the flaws, or at least to decrease the negative consequences of them.*

Actually, this explanation of S2 in Chapter 6 was derived from the separate level descriptions of S2. Here they are:

Example: levels of a generic competence

Competence S: Systems orientation
A sustainably competent professional thinks and acts from a systemic perspective.

Achievement S2:
Recognize flaws in the fabric and sources of vigor in systems; have the ability to use the sources of vigor

Level 3: Apply
- You analyze the structure of your immediate working environment.
- Based on this, you make a SWOT analysis.

Level 4: Integrate
- You make this SWOT analysis for the organization of which you are a member and its surroundings.
- You do so from a perspective of sustainable development, for example from the *Triple P.*

Level 5: Improve
- You make the SWOT analysis in close collaboration with representatives from all levels of your organization.
- Based on the SWOT analysis you formulate recommendations to use strengths and opportunities, to improve weaknesses and to anticipate on threats.

Level 6: Innovate
- You make the SWOT analysis also in close collaboration with representatives in the wide surroundings of your organization.
- You make recommendations to strengthen the structure of the system considerably.

Together, the descriptions of the various levels for all eighteen (6 x 3) achievements form a *Set of Competence Cards*, a reference map that can be used to assess the competences of individual professionals.

If you are interested in seeing the entire set, just download it here and hit the hyperlink to the pdf file:

https://niko.roorda.nu/management-methods/resfia-d.

DISCIPLINARY COMPETENCE LEVELS

As you know from Chapter 11, an infinitely large set of disciplinary competences exists due to the fact that there is an unlimited and ever-growing number of professions. If you wanted to define concrete competence levels for some of them, you would first have to develop a valid set of competences that are specific to a certain profession.

This is what I did in 2016, as a part of a Europe-wide project aiming at developing a set of sustainability competences for *educators*. The project was funded by the European Commission. After studying relevant sources and discussing the topic with the members of the international project team, I defined a set of Educator Competences for Sustainable Development. By coincidence, this set consists of three achievements, just like the six generic competences. This is not a necessity; for other professions, the number might just as well be different. Anyway, the three achievements are:

+D for Educators:

D1 Innovate education, regarding structures, methods, and contents
D2 Offer challenging, learner-centered education within real-life contexts
D3 Involve sustainable development in learner assessments

After these three achievements were defined, it became possible to develop the competence level descriptions. As an example, I offer you D2.

Example: levels of a disciplinary competence

Competence D: Educator competence
A sustainably competent educator involves sustainable development in his or her professional activities wherever it makes sense.

Achievement D2:
Offer challenging, learner-centered education within real-life contexts

Level 3: Apply
- You apply a variety of pedagogic and didactic methods, enabling the learners to understand the basic notions of sustainable development.
- You also stimulate learners to discover the relations between sustainable development and their own (present or future) neighborhood and/or profession.

Level 4: Integrate
- You guide learners to discover the relations between sustainable development and all topics in the curriculum, causing sustainable development to be a continuous thread or fundament throughout the curriculum.
- Doing this, you enable the learners to act in a multidisciplinary way.
- You enable the learners to act within a real-life context, or at least within a realistic context.

Level 5: Improve
- Feedback from learners, colleagues and experts is used by you to systematically improve the learning process and your role in it.
- Topical developments are constantly observed by you, and used to keep the learning process up to date.

Level 6: Innovate
- You cooperate with colleagues from different topics, and with external experts, in order to let the learners operate in an interdisciplinary or even transdisciplinary context.
- Doing this, you show leadership among your colleagues and all others who are involved in the learning process in an educating capacity.

Let me now move to the three ways in which RESFIA+D can be applied as an assessment tool.

14.2 INDIVIDUAL PROFESSIONALS: PERSONAL DEVELOPMENT PLAN

The first and easiest application is by an individual professional. It might be you, a colleague, a supervisor, a member of your staff, or an intern. Students can do it, as a part of their study program in a university, a college, or a school.

The assessment can be done repeatedly, for instance every one, two, or three years, as a part of a cyclic professional development process.

STEP 1: YOUR PRESENT COMPETENCE, ACCORDING TO YOURSELF

First, you go through all six generic competences one by one; and for each of them you go through the three achievements that are defined.

If, as a preparation, a set of disciplinary competences has been defined for your profession (e.g. by an expert group, by the organization you work for, or by you), you include those as well.

For each of these 18 or more achievements, you sincerely ask yourself, after reading the detailed level descriptions: do I really do this, or at least do I do things that are comparable with these descriptions? At which level do I do it?

Don't fool yourself by being too optimistic; why would you?

STEP 2: FEEDBACK FROM OTHERS

Next, you invite one or more persons who are familiar with you and your work and whom you trust to score the 18 or more topics with you in mind. If enough people do this, you get a 360° feedback.

Of course, if you cannot or don't want to get this kind of feedback, you can leave Step 2 out.

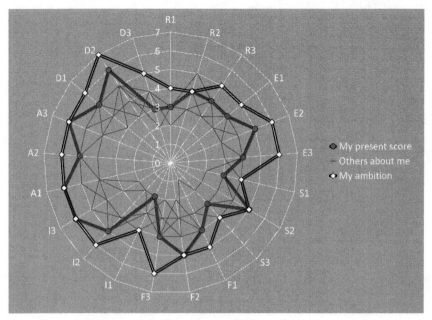

Figure 14.1 *A RESFIA+D result of an individual professional*

STEP 3: YOUR AMBITION

Then, you define your ambition for each of the topics. Before you do, you might select a certain period of time in which you want to realize this ambition: i.e. a target date. The result may look like Figure 14.1, which is an actual result, scored a few years ago by a Dutch professional working as a consultant.

STEP 4: PERSONAL DEVELOPMENT PLAN

After you complete the assessment, you use the results to think about how you can realize your ambition. This includes things like setting priorities, selecting methods to improve your competence levels (e.g. reading a book, doing an internship, participating in a training course, playing a serious game, investigating internet pages), and finding facilities to do this (e.g. time, money, equipment, teachers, permissions).

14.3 ORGANIZATIONS: HUMAN RESOURCE DEVELOPMENT (HRD)

If you work in a company, it may be decided that not only you but also others perform an individual RESFIA+D assessment. Perhaps all the members of a certain team will participate: the consultants, the teachers, the doctors or nurses, the financial staff, the salespersons, and the top managers.

STEP 1: MINIMUM ACCEPTABLE LEVEL

As a preparation, a *minimum requirement* can be defined. This is a set of 18 (or more, if disciplinary competences were defined) levels that are the lowest acceptable level for anyone within the team.

STEP 2: AMBITION LEVEL

At the other end, also an *ambition level* is defined for the entire team. This does not require *every* team member to meet the demands of this ambition; it involves the combined strength of the team as a whole. It may e.g. be decided that all ambition levels need to be possessed by at least one or two team members; if not, the team may not be able to perform its tasks properly.

STEP 3: INDIVIDUAL ASSESSMENTS

All team members – or at least those who were selected for the assessment – do the assessment, as described in 14.2. In this case, the 360° feedback should definitely not be left out!

After the individual assessments are finished, the result may look like Figure 14.2.

STEP 4: STAFF DEVELOPMENT PLAN

Based on this result, the team – or its managers – will develop a *Staff Development Plan*. This plan describes how the team is going to meet

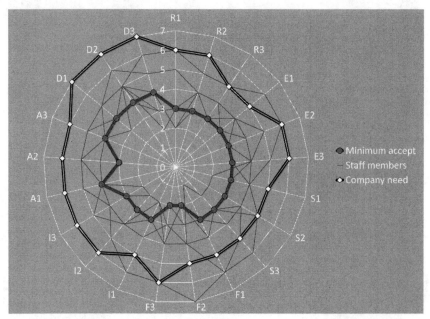

Figure 14.2 *A RESFIA+D result of an organization*

the formulated ambition within a limited period of time, e.g. a year. This may be based on negotiations with individual team members, resulting in agreements that certain members will follow courses, perhaps in-company, while others will find different ways to develop themselves. For those team members who don't meet the minimum demands, such a development plan is especially important; if it were to fail, it might ultimately lead to a dismissal procedure.

14.4 UNIVERSITIES & COLLEGES: CURRICULUM DEVELOPMENT

RESFIA+D has also proved to be valuable for educational institutions, especially for study programs and their curricula. You can think of scientific and vocational education in universities, colleges, and schools.

The method has been used for a wide variety of disciplines, e.g. technological, economic, social, agricultural, healthcare, law, and teacher education.

If a curriculum is to be (re)designed, this process should always start at the end, that is by (re)defining the outcomes of the study program, formulated as a set of competences of the graduates. This is where RESFIA+D comes in. When the competence profile is defined in a proper way, the curriculum contents as well as the curriculum structure and didactic methods can be derived from it.

STEP 1: COMPOSING AN ASSESSMENT GROUP

As a preparation for the assessment, a group of circa ten to 15 people is formed. Together, they have to be representative of all those who are stakeholders of the study program.

Another demand for each of the group members is that they are sufficiently familiar with the current curriculum or, if no curriculum exists yet, with the demands of the professional field and of society in general in relation to the study program.

The group will consist of: lecturers, professors; learners, students; program managers, deans and/or even the institution board; recent alumni (with a fresh memory of the entire study program) – unless the program is brand new; and experienced representatives of the academic or professional field the study program aims at.

In some cases, also: representatives of society in general, e.g. community leaders; education financers; representatives of special interest groups, e.g. minorities or the environment.

STEP 2: CREATING CONSENSUS ON PRESENT STATE AND AMBITION

The group meets only once, for half a day or a few hours more. At the beginning, the assessor (someone who is highly experienced in applying

RESFIA+D for this purpose) explains the goals and structure of the assessment method and the purpose of the meeting.

Next, the assessor goes through all 18 achievements of the 'RESFIA' part, i.e. the generic competences, one by one. If disciplinary competences were defined beforehand, they are applied as well. For each of the 18 or more achievements, the assessor asks three questions, which the group discusses until consensus is reached.

The questions are:

1   For this specific achievement, which is the minimum competence level each student should *at least* have acquired when graduating? (the *ambition*)
2   Which is the level that is demanded in the present *competence profile?*
3   And which level is actually *realized* by each and every graduate at the very least?

In many cases, the answers to those three questions may be different. It is not uncommon that the group concludes that the ambition for a certain achievement should be, for example, Level 6; while the profile of the program demands perhaps Level 5, and the level that is actually realized, at least by some graduates, may be Level 4.

The overall result may look like Figure 14.3, which was an actual result of the assessment of a study program (Bachelor of Commerce) in 2014.

STEP 3: SELECTING PRIORITIES

After the group has reached consensus on the answers to the three questions for all 18 or more achievements, its task is nearly finished. What remains is setting priorities for an improvement project.

You see, the strength of the assessment is that it is not an external expert who is going to tell the study program team that *their program is not good enough*. If there are differences between the ambitions and the present state – and there always are – it is the members of the group,

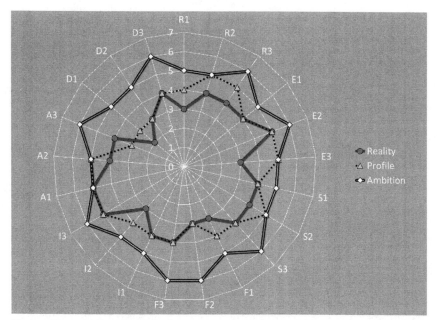

Figure 14.3 *A RESFIA+D result of a university curriculum*

including those who are responsible for the program, who draw the conclusions. They themselves determine the necessary improvements; they are the ones who give themselves a task. *They own the conclusions.*

On the other hand, there may perhaps be as many as 15 or more improvements that are to be realized. But you probably know that any plan with more than – say – three to five main goals is bound to fail. That is why it is important to select a limited set of highest priorities, out of all suggested improvements. Usually this appears to be an easy task. Each desired improvement has been discussed in detail. The group will probably know already, which of them are crucial first steps, and which others will follow easily as a result of the crucial first improvements.

Selecting the priorities is usually done in ten minutes.

The result, which is to be turned into a report, formally has a status of *recommendations to the management*. Of course, the management is likely to accept and embrace these recommendations since they participated in the discussions, and the conclusions were drawn in consensus. It's a truly democratic process, creating a lot of support and enthusiasm.

STEP 4: EDUCATION DEVELOPMENT PLAN

The final step will be for the management, i.e. for those people who carry the responsibility for the quality of the study program.

Preferably, the management team meets the very next day, when memories of the assessment are still fresh. During this meeting, the set of recommendations is turned into a solid *Education Development Plan*.

This plan arranges how and when the current competence profile is adapted, followed by the necessary changes to the curriculum. The plan will involve a time schedule, a budget, the responsibilities of those who are going to do the actual work, their facilities, etc.

It will also contain an overview of the competences the education team will need to develop the improved program and to teach it. Consequently, a new staff development plan may be necessary, if not all necessary competences are present within the team. If so, RESFIA+D may again be useful, this time along the lines of Section 14.3, above.

After the plan is constructed, a period follows in which it is executed. At the end of this period, another round may follow in which RESFIA+D is applied again, leading to new conclusions, and so on. In this way, a quality circle is closed.

14.5 AND NOW SOME ACTION: THE SELF-TEST

Dear reader, I am certain that you have wondered about your own personal competence profile a few times while reading this book. Probably, you have compared some of these stories to your own experiences in your career. Would you have acted similarly, had you been in the same circumstances as the professionals featured here? Maybe you actually do things that are comparable with the actions of the professionals in this book. How about your ambitions? Would you perhaps aspire to reaching the master level of sustainability competence?

PERSONAL GROWTH TOWARD SUSTAINABLE MASTERSHIP

In Chapter 7, I wrote about levels of competence. For your convenience, here they are again.

Level 1:	Apprentice
Level 2:	Work under supervision
Level 3:	Self-direct
Level 4:	Integrate
Level 5:	Improve
Level 6:	Innovate
Level 7:	Master

It stands to reason that nobody will ever attain absolute mastership in every aspect. Universal masters don't exist. You can be a master in one area while being a fool or a novice in another. Life is a process of growth that doesn't end with official retirement as the example of retired social worker Merle Wexler, who continues to volunteer, demonstrates in Chapter 11.

THE SELF-TEST

The self-test is an easy way to apply RESFIA+D as an individual professional, as described in Section 14.2. In the form below, you can insert your personal level for each of the RESFIA+D competences. If you are in doubt about the exact meaning of a particular competence, you can review the story describing the competence in one of the earlier chapters. If you want to learn more about the background of the competences and how they relate to sustainable development and corporate social responsibility (CSR), you can read more about them in my book *Fundamentals of Sustainable Development*. In the form below, I added a column referring to the appropriate sections in that book.

If you want, you can download the detailed level descriptions for each achievement, as I mentioned in Section 14.1. If you don't want to do that, you can estimate the contents of the levels in a more intuitive way.

Below, you can fill out three columns. In the first, you insert your personal scores, based on your own judgment and feelings. (Of course, you may insert very high scores everywhere if that makes you happy, but whom are you really fooling?)

In order to compare your personal judgment to the observations of others, you can ask one or more trusted persons to complete the second column. If you wish, you can even turn this into a parlor game by discussing all of your personal competences with a group of people and determine the scores together.

The right column represents your wish list. Select a concrete moment in the future that is meaningful to you, for instance, one, three, or ten years from now. What sort of professional do you want to be by then? What are your ambitions?

The bottom of the form is about **D**, i.e. the disciplinary competences. Of course, I cannot determine those for you. Therefore, you will find a number of empty boxes into which you can write the competences you consider relevant. I reserved room for six such competences, but you may expand the list beyond that, of course. However, don't go too far. . .

The RESFIA+D self-test

R: Responsibility A sustainably competent professional bears responsibility for his or her own work.	Explanation (Fundamentals of Sustainable development)	Your level (According to you)	Your level (According to trusted person)	Your ambition
R1 Create a stakeholder analysis on the basis of the consequence scope and the consequence period	5.5			
R2 Take personal responsibility	8.2			
R3 Be held personally accountable with respect to society (transparency)	8.2			

E: Emotional intelligence A sustainably competent professional empathizes with the values and emotions of others.	Explanation (Fundamentals of Sustainable development)	Your level (According to you)	Your level (According to trusted person)	Your ambition
E1 Recognize and respect his or her own values and those of other people and cultures	4.3			
E2 Distinguish between facts, assumptions, and opinions	8.5			
E3 Cooperate on an interdisciplinary and transdisciplinary basis	1.3, 4.8			

S: Systems orientation A sustainably competent professional thinks and acts from a systemic perspective.	Explanation (Fundamentals of Sustainable development)	Your level (According to you)	Your level (According to trusted person)	Your ambition
S1 Think from systems: flexibly zoom in and out on issues, i.e. thinking analytically and holistically in turn	3.5			
S2 Recognize flaws in the fabric and sources of vigor in systems; have the ability to use the sources of vigor	Chapters 2–4			
S3 Think integrally and chain-oriented	8.3			

F: Future orientation A sustainably competent professional thinks and acts on the basis of a perspective of the future.	Explanation (Fundamentals of Sustainable development)	Your level (According to you)	Your level (According to trusted person)	Your ambition
F1 Think on different time scales – flexibly zoom in and out on short- and long-term approaches	5.5			
F2 Recognize and utilize non-linear processes	7.3			
F3 Think innovatively, creatively, and out of the box	8.4			

I: personal Involvement

A sustainably competent professional has a personal involvement in sustainable development.

Explanation (Fundamentals of Sustainable development)	Your level (According to you)	Your level (According to trusted person)	Your ambition
I1 Consistently involve sustainable development in his or her own work as a professional (sustainable attitude)	4.7		
I2 Passionately work toward dreams and ideals	4.2		
I3 Employ his or her conscience as the ultimate yardstick	8.2		

A: Action skills

A sustainably competent professional is decisive and capable of acting.

Explanation (Fundamentals of Sustainable development)	Your level (According to you)	Your level (According to trusted person)	Your ambition
A1 Weigh up the unweighable and make decisions	8.5		
A2 Deal with uncertainties	6.3		
A3 Act when the time is right, and do not go against the current: "action without action"	4.2		

D: Disciplinary competences *Add competences that are linked to your discipline and/or profession.*	Your level *(According to you)*	Your level *(According to trusted person)*	Your ambition
D1			
D2			
D3			
D4			
D5			
D6			

You can insert your scores in the empty diagram of Figure 14.4, if you wish.

If your ambitions exceed your present scores – and I hope they do because who does not want to improve? – then think of a plan to make your ambitions come true. Who knows? Maybe, within a couple of years you may have excellently mastered (certain aspects of) sustainable development. Anyway, you don't have to be a master to be able to act as a sustainably competent professional, as this book has shown.

14.6 THE PLEDGE

Finally, medical doctors have their Hippocratic Oath, which they pledge during their graduation ceremony at the end of their academic education program. This is for good reason since they are

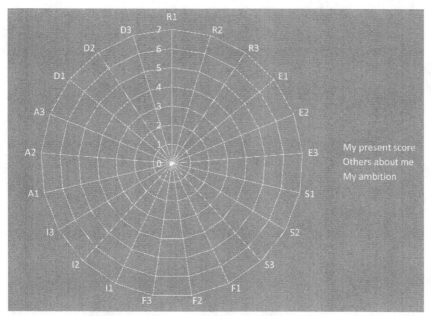

Figure 14.4 *An empty RESFIA+D graph, to be used for the self-test*

about to start their professional careers, during which, with some regularity, they – or at least some of them – will have the lives of their patients in their hands. Those are responsible professionals!

And others? Those of us who are not medical specialists? They, too, hold the lives of others in their hands, albeit in a more figurative sense: the lives of humans, of animals, or of nature in general. Managers may support or crush the careers of their employees, and so may teachers in the course of the school lives or university programs of young individuals. Engineers design products in such a way that they may destroy or strengthen the natural environment. Caretakers make the lives of their clients bearable – or not. Artists represent the conscience of society – or they don't. Aren't those responsible professions too? I think they are.

Hence my question: do you have the courage to make a pledge, promising you will behave as a responsible and sustainably competent professional?

Information about the pledge is available on my website, at https://niko. roorda.nu/pledge.

You can make your pledge to your husband or wife. To your children, your forefathers, your colleagues, the Bible, the *Quran*, the Bhagavad Gita, your stamp collection, or whatever is sacred to you. Legally binding it will not be. Morally binding it is.

> *Pledge*
>
> *I promise that in my work I will consistently consider the consequences of my actions for society and for the environment, both today and in the future. I shall, before making decisions and whilst making them, conscientiously assess issues. I shall not undertake any actions geared toward harming people or the natural environment. I shall use my education, talents and experiences in order to make a contribution to a better world through sustainable development.*
>
> *I accept that I am personally responsible for my choices and actions, and I promise that I will be held publicly accountable for my work by everyone for whom that work holds consequences. I shall not appeal to the fact that I acted on the instructions of others.*
>
> *I promise that in my work I will not only make an effort for my own interests and my career, but also for my dreams and my ideals. In this I shall respect the values and the interests of others.*
>
> *I understand that there will be times in the course of my career when it will be difficult to do what I am now promising to do. I will adhere to this pledge, even in those times.*

REFERENCES AND WEBLINKS

INTRODUCTION

Carolina Machado (University of Minho, Portugal) and J. Paulo Davim (University of Aveiro, Portugal): 'Management for Sustainable Development'. River Publishers, Denmark, 2015, ISBN 9788793379084: Chapter 1, pages 1–48.

CHAPTER 1

RESFIA+D: https://niko.roorda.nu/management-methods/resfia-d

CHAPTER 2

Amnesty International: www.amnestyusa.org
Foster Parents Plan: https://plan-international.org
Cordaid: www.cordaid.org/en
World Wildlife Fund (WWF): www.worldwildlife.org
International Union for the Conservation of Nature (IUCN):
    www.iucn.org
City of Redmond: www.redmond.gov
Muslim Association of Puget Sound (MAPS): www.youtube.com/
    watch?v=jj29FTlds9Q
DSM: www.dsm.com
Children's Investment Fund Foundation: http://ciff.org

Millennium Development Goals (MDGs): www.un.org/millenniumgoals
The MDGs were valid from 2000 until 2015 and have now ended. They
    have been followed up by the Sustainable Development Goals (SDGs),
    valid for 2015 till 2030: https://sustainabledevelopment.un.org/sdgs
Troféu Curuca de Sustentabilidade: www.feedfood.com.br/
    trofeu-curuca-premia-empresas-que-se-destacaram-com-acoes-
    de-sustentabilidade-durante-ano-de-2012
Global Reporting Initiative (GRI): www.globalreporting.org/Pages/
    default.aspx
Dow Jones Sustainability Index (DJSI): www.sustainability-indices.com
ISO 26000: www.iso.org/iso/home/standards/iso26000.htm

CHAPTER 4

Transition Towns: www.transitionnetwork.org
Transition Town Totnes: www.transitiontowntotnes.org
Transition Towns USA: http://transitionus.org
Transition Towns California: www.transitiontownsca.org
Transition Towns Woodstock: http://woodstocknytransition.org

CHAPTER 5

Brundtland Report: download from: www.un-documents.net/ocf-ov.htm
Ismael Serageldin, 1996: "Sustainability and the wealth of nations.
    First steps in an ongoing journey". Environmentally Sustainable
    Development Studies and Monograph Series 5, World Bank,
    Washington DC, 1996. Download from: www.serageldin.com/
    Attachment/EuPy2fGQJx_20150218130008191.pdf

CHAPTER 6

Permaculture: www.permacultureintl.com
Permaculture in Oregon (Andrew Millison): http://horticulture.
    oregonstate.edu/content/andrew-millison

Permaculture education: www.permaculturerising.com
Grounds for Health: www.groundsforhealth.org
Floow2: www.floow2.com
Pay per lux (Philips, Thoma Rau): www.ellenmacarthurfoundation.org/
    case-studies/selling-light-as-a-service

CHAPTER 8

National Oceanic and Atmospheric Association (NOAA): www.noaa.gov
CropMobster: http://sfbay.cropmobster.com
Maslow's pyramid: Maslow, A (1954). Motivation and personality. New
    York, NY: Harper. ISBN 0-06-041987-3. https://en.wikipedia.org/wiki/
    Maslow's_hierarchy_of_needs
Function Analysis: https://niko.roorda.nu/management-methods/
    de-tgo-tools/functieanalyse-function-analysis/#Introduction

CHAPTER 10

Fight for Light: http://fightforlight.org
Student Outreach and Retention Center for Equity (SORCE)
    at the University of Colorado Boulder: www.youtube.com/
    watch?v=eoFFBcR2ozI
Speakers Academy: www.speakersacademy.com/en/speaker/niko-
    roorda

CHAPTER 11

Be Green Packaging: www.begreenpackaging.com
Vancity: www.vancity.com
Global Alliance for Banking on Values: www.gabv.org
Teo Castellanos: www.teocastellanos.com
EY (Ernst & Young): www.ey.com
Leisha John on *White roofs for green schools*: www.youtube.com/
    watch?v=eHK8Evlq44Q

Ecovative: www.ecovativedesign.com. Eben Bayer: www.ted.com/talks/
    eben_bayer_are_mushrooms_the_new_plastic?language=en
Organic Valley Co-op: www.organicvalley.coop
The Land Institute: https://landinstitute.org
Guardian ad Litem: www.guardianadlitem.org
University of Florida, Division of Infectious Diseases & Global Medicine:
    http://id.medicine.ufl.edu
Air Base K-8 Center, Homestead, Florida: www.airbasek8.net
Nurturing Environmental Stewards of Today and Tomorrow (NESTT):
    www.deeringestate.org/nestt

CHAPTER 12

PAX: www.paxforpeace.nl
International Criminal Court (ICC): www.icc-cpi.int
Documentary 'Kony 2012' on YouTube: www.youtube.com/
    watch?v=Y4MnpzG5Sqc
The Natural Step: www.naturalstep.ca
ISL Engineering and Land Services: www.islengineering.com
Journal of Daoist Studies: www.daoiststudies.org
Montclair Kimberley Academy: www.mka.org
Wei wu wei: http://ccbs.ntu.edu.tw/FULLTEXT/JR-PHIL/loy3.htm

CHAPTER 13

Color schemes of the Candoshi and the Kwerba: "Color
    Naming Across Languages", Paul Kay et al, Cambridge
    1997. Download from: http://citeseerx.ist.psu.edu/viewdoc/
    download;jsessionid=3944F8C981C57B8A4206C2348CC612C2?doi=
    10.1.1.40.6516&rep=rep1&type=pdf

CHAPTER 14

Niko Roorda: Fundamentals of sustainable development, www.routledge.
    com/cw/roorda-9781849713863
The Pledge: ditto, and also: https://niko.roorda.nu/the-pledge

GLOSSARY

Active listening Not just hearing what others say, but also trying to understand what they intend. Active listening skills enable you to indicate that you are listening, to allow others to tell their stories, and, whenever necessary, to let them clarify

Anticipate Look far ahead into the future and act accordingly in order to be prepared for it

Consequence period The time it takes before the consequences of a decision have disappeared

Consequence scope The totality of all the people, organizations, animals, and the environment that experience the consequences of a given decision, behavior, or lifestyle

Disciplinary From or within a certain discipline

Discipline The subject area in which you work and (probably) have expertise in, e.g. mechanical engineering, economics, nursing, etc.

Expertise Combination of knowledge, insight, skills, and attitude (together abbreviated as "KISA"). It may be based on theoretical, formal learning as well as on practical experiences

Habitat The natural environment of a plant or an animal species, or a complex combination of them

Interdisciplinary A way of cooperating in a team that involves experts of various disciplines so that productive, creative, innovative strategies and methods can be developed and used

KISA   Description of four kinds of professional tools or capabilities; an acronym for Knowledge = what you know, Insight = what you understand, Skills = what you are able to do, and Attitude = who you are

Line of business   Working sector in which you have a job, e.g. metallurgical industry, accountancy, health, or education

Linear   Literally: straight-lined; linear consequences are directly proportional to their causes. (See: non-linear consequences)

Mission   Fundamental principles and objectives of an organization, the reason why it exists; often made explicit in a "mission statement"

Monodisciplinary   An approach in which a project or a problem is viewed from the perspective of just one discipline

Multidisciplinary   An approach in which a problem is viewed from the perspectives of various disciplines, allowing different angles and methods; the experts are not in intensive contact with each other, making it unlikely that solutions based on combinations of disciplines will be developed

Non-linear consequences   Consequences that are not directly proportional to the causes and which can have unexpected effects

Operational methods   Methods that can be applied immediately or on short notice, possibly but not necessarily, on the basis of tactical or strategic plans

Participation   Taking part in activities, processes, groups, or society in general as an accepted, valued, and self-aware member

People   One of the three main 'pillars' of sustainable development, concerning topics like culture, human rights, participation, education, health, and empowerment

Planet   One of the three main 'pillars' of sustainable development, concerning topics like biodiversity, environment, nature, and climate

Precautionary principle   The idea that policy decisions are based (at least partially) on the prevention of certain negative consequences, even if the occurrence of these negative consequences is not certain

Profit   One of the three 'pillars' of sustainable development, concerning topics like investments, profitability, economic stability, and GDP

Prosperity   An alternative for the term "profit," with a more inclusive meaning, also related to the economic position of individuals, families, and local communities

RESFIA+D   A scheme of six general professional competences for sustainable development, each consisting of three more detailed competences, plus disciplinary competences that differ for educational programs or professional groups

Scenario   A scenario of a play or movie is a description of the scenes that make up the story. A future scenario is a description of the developments that might take place in a possible future

Stakeholder   A person or group that has an interest in certain discussions, events, decisions, or developments

Stakeholder analysis   The process of investigating all those who have an interest in a certain project, process, or company, and who would be affected in both a positive or negative sense

Strategic policy   A long-term policy, aiming at the realization of fundamental goals, based on the mission of an organization or redefining these goals or the mission

Sustainable   Capable of lasting long

Sustainable development   Development that leads to a situation in which an increasing part of humanity can live an acceptable life, in such a way that future generations will be able to do the same

Tactical policy   An intermediate-term policy, aiming at the realization of the concrete goals of an organization, possibly but not necessarily, on the basis of tactical or strategic plans

Transdisciplinary   A way of cooperating as an interdisciplinary team that includes not only experts from a certain discipline but also persons who have practical experience in the particular field or who otherwise have an interest

Trend   The direction into which a certain development is moving over a relatively long period

ABOUT THE AUTHORS

DR. NIKO ROORDA (1955) is one of the international pioneers in the area of education and sustainable development (ESD), working full-time on the topic since 1991.

First, he developed the university program of Sustainable Technology, acting as the manager and one of the lecturers. Next, he designed and chaired an intensive program with the aim of integrating SD into a wide range of academic programs. He also developed a program on Sustainable Entrepreneurship.

For the past 15 years, Roorda has worked as a consultant, coaching ESD strategies to more than 50 universities and companies on four continents and offering lectures and training programs. He has developed a range of management tools and assessment instruments. Some of them are in use in more than 30 countries. One of them is the *RESFIA+D* model for SD competences, which is the fundament of *The Seven Competences of the Sustainable Professional.*

Born in the Netherlands, Roorda studied Astronomy (BSc), Theoretical Physics, and Philosophy (MSc). With a dissertation based on his decades-long work on ESD, he received his Ph.D. in the social sciences in 2010.

The Seven Competences of the Sustainable Professional is Roorda's tenth book about SD and CSR (corporate social responsibility). One of his other works is the university textbook *Fundamentals of Sustainable Development* (2nd edition, Routledge, 2017). He has also written many articles and chapters in journals and books.

For his achievements, Roorda received the Dutch National Award for Innovation and Sustainable Development, awarded by the Ministries of Environmental Management and of Education of the Netherlands.

Roorda's personal website is https://niko.roorda.nu.

DR. ANOUCHKA RACHELSON (1966), Professor of English for Academic Purposes in the department of World Languages at Miami Dade College (MDC), Florida, combines her love of language with her passion for the environment in her research and teaching. She has published articles on sustainability education in *The Journal of Sustainability Education* and regularly incorporates sustainability issues in her curricula, both as a pedagogical tool and to stimulate environmental awareness among her students.

Having served on MDC's Earth Ethics Institute Council since 2006, Dr. Rachelson creates professional development workshops on sustainability in higher education for faculty and also facilitates graduate courses on sustainability education. She has been instrumental in designing and implementing MDC's Global Sustainability and Earth Literacy Studies (GSELS) program, which "explores global citizenship, ecological sustainability, and civic engagement, through understanding planetary challenges and limits and by developing values, skills, and behaviors that promote prosperity and communities of well-being" (earthethicsinstitute.org).

A native of Berlin, Dr. Rachelson studied English (BA) and teaching English to students of other languages (MSc). She has taught at Miami Dade College since 2002, and prior to that worked as an ESL and German instructor in Japan. In 2010, she earned her doctorate in higher education from Florida International University. In her dissertation, Dr.

Rachelson analyzed the attitudes, beliefs, and practices of community college professors regarding sustainable development.

For her excellence in teaching, Professor Rachelson was honored with MDC's Dr. Eduardo Padrón Endowed Teaching Chair Award in 2015.

ABOUT THIS BOOK

The Seven Competences of the Sustainable Professional is the American edition of a book by Roorda that was published in the Dutch language in 2015. The framework of the Dutch book was applied again in the American edition; most of the American and Canadian cases have been gathered and written by co-author Anouchka Rachelson.

ACKNOWLEDGMENTS

The authors wish to thank their spouses Marjo and Carl for their support and patience, and the following persons for their wonderful contributions to this book:

Contributor	Sector	Organization	Function	Topic
Andrew Millison	Design	Permaculture Design International	Designer and Instructor	Permaculture design
Amy Yomiko Vittor	Medical research	University of Florida	Professor	Vector-borne diseases
Brian Cade	Banking	Vancity	Account Manager	Sustainable investment
David Hessler	Education	Montclair Kimberley Academy	Educator	Action without action
Eben Bayer	Industry	Ecovative	CEO and Founder	Cradle 2 Cradle design
Eva Van Wingerden	Industry	Be Green Packaging	Eco Social Director	Zero waste production
Gary Mosgaller	Agriculture	Organic Valley	Dairy Farmer	Conventional to organic
Genevieve Maignan-Keogh	Counseling	Public High School	School Counselor	Conflict resolution
Hannah Purcell	Education	Air Base K-8 Center	School Teacher	Raise love for nature
Herman Betten	Chemistry	DSM	Communication manager	Transparency
Hyder Ali	Spirituality	Muslim Ass. of Puget Sound	Founding President, Board Member	Acting responsibly
Jan Gruiters	Development	IKV PAX Christi	Director	Negotiating with war criminals
Jenny Parren	Retail	Clothing store	Store Manager	Conscience
John Jordan	Consultancy	Fight for Light	Social Entrepreneur	Sustainable attitude
Kirk Ritchey	Community	Transition Town Woodstock	Core Organizer	Collaboration
Koos Spee	Traffic	VerkeerDeBaas	Public Prosecutor	Non-linear traffic
Leisha John	Consultancy	EY (Ernst & Young)	Envir. Sustainability Director	Develop a sustainability strategy
Merle Wexler	Social work	Guardian ad Litem	Social Worker	Advocating for children

Contributor	Sector	Organization	Function	Topic
Nick Papadopoulos	Agriculture	CropMobster	Co-owner	Food waste and community
Pong Leung	Consultancy	The Natural Step	Senior Associate	Deal with uncertainties, Backcasting
Ricci Silberman	Healthcare	Grounds for Health	Family Practitioner	Sustainable medicine
Sandra Veenstra	Mental Health	Veenstra Psychology	Psychologist	Chronic fatigue
Simone Lopulisa	Banking	A bank	Advisor	Crowd sourcing
Susy Torriente	Government	City of Miami Beach	Chief Resiliency Officer	Short- and long-term
Teo Castellanos	Culture	Teo Castellanos	Actor/Director/Writer	Inspire social change
Vita Vanderbilt	Healthcare	Hospital	Nurse	Child abuse
Will Robben	Production	Floow2	Entrepreneur	From product to service

PHOTO CREDIT

Planet Earth, shown as a photo in the bottom part of the image about a circular economy in Chapter 6, is made by NASA Headquarters – Greatest Images of NASA (NASA-HQ-GRIN).

INDEX